A.G. RUSSELL'S KNIFE TRADER'S GUIDE

A. G. RUSSELL & GOLDIE RUSSELL

PAUL WAHL Corporation

A. G. RUSSELL'S
KNIFE TRADER'S GUIDE

ISBN 0-943997-25-9

Suggested retail price US $10

Published by
Paul Wahl Corporation
Bogota, NJ 07603-0500
Cut 'n Shoot, TX 77303-7000

About This Book

HAVE YOU EVER NOTICED all of the people who trudge about knife shows uncomfortably clutching phone-book size value guides under their arms? This suggested a pressing need for the pocketable *Knife Trader's Guide*. It differs from other knife price books in content as well as format. These prices are real—not somebody's guesstimates of current market values. Listed are actual prices received by A. G. Russell in thousands of recent sales of popular collectible knives.

Generally, knife values are pretty stable. However, some hot items do skyrocket. Recent examples include the Benchmark Rolox and Gerber Paul knives that have more than quadrupled in value in just two years. Keep an eye on such collectibles.

The prices in *Knife Trader's Guide* are at current retail level. When you're selling to a dealer, remember that he has overhead and must make a decent profit on resale. Don't be surprised if you are offered 50% of these prices. On consignments, the dealer probably will ask for a 25% to 35% commission.

Knowing what a knife is really worth is a must when you're dealing. Always have *Knife Trader's Guide* handy in your hip pocket.

Recent Sales Prices of Popular Collectible Knives

All knives listed, when sold by A. G. Russell, were in unused condition, straight knives had sheaths, unless otherwise indicated.

A

AERIAL CUTLERY CO. Two-blade senator, nickel silver bolsters, brass liners, jigged bone scales $40

AGEE Drop point, 4" blade, nickel silver hilt and pins, buffalo horn scales, early work by very talented maker $165

AGEE Drop point, 3½" stainless steel blade and hilt, mortise tang, burgundy Micarta handle $165

AITOR (SPAIN) 8½" bush, wood Micarta handle $65

AITOR (SPAIN) 3" blade, all steel skeleton $20

ALASKA CANNON 6¼" blade, brass hilt, pins and thong hole, wood slabs, used $100

ALEXANDER (SHEFFIELD) Old dagger, 5" blade, nickel silver hilt, stag scales, NY shield inlay, good shape considering age, no sheath $155

ALVERSON, TIM 3⅞" knife and fork set, integral bolsters and stainless butts, sterling-wire-wrapped oosic handles $355

AMERICAN BLADE Midlock three-blade whittler, 3½" closed, nickel silver bolsters, brass liners, bone stag scales, American Blade Collectors 1983 #3008 $45

AMERICAN BLADE Three-blade dog-leg stock, 3½" closed, nickel silver bolsters, brass liners, black pearl scales, 1984 Collectors Edition, serial #531 .... $65

ANDERSON, G. Bootknife, 5¼" blade, brass bolster and butt, rosewood handle, no sheath $65

ANDREWS ERA II, 4⅛" closed lockback, nickel silver frames, desert ironwood scales, his first folder $170

ANKROM Bowie, 8⅛" flat-ground hand-rubbed blade, nickel silver hilt, mortise tang, African Blackwood handle, a very fine knife, no sheath $565

ANKROM Hunter, 5⅛" flat ground blade, hand-rubbed nickel silver hilt, India stag handle ... $275

ANKROM Lockback, 3¼" closed, nickel silver bolsters and caps, ivory scales $200

ANKROM Lockback, 3¼" closed, nickel silver bolsters, caps and liners, mother of pearl $285

ANKROM Lockback, 4⅜" closed, nickel silver bolsters, liners, exhibition grade pearl # 180 .... $265

ANKROM Lockback, 5½" closed, nickel silver bolsters, satin finish blade, cocobolo $355

ANKROM Lockback bootknife, 4¼" closed, nickel silver liners and bolsters, matched stag scales $295

ANKROM/SHAW-LIEBOWITZ Dagger letter-opener, 4" blade, very fancy cast sterling silver handle, vermeil lion at hilt, glass topped display box $295

ANTIQUE Blade marked AR, late 18th or early 19th century (believed to be 1812 war relic), horn handles, very used $125

ANTIQUE Folding knife and fork set, (15th or 16th century), German silver, amber, engraved, very nice mint condition $695

ANTIQUE Folding scalpel, 3⅝" closed, four locking blades, tortoise shell scales (one broken), finest and most unusual antique scalpel I have seen $185

ANTIQUE H & B Mfg. Co., slipjoint hunter, 5¾" closed, iron bolsters and caps, brass liners, cocobolo scales, very unusual late 19th or early 20th century, good to very good condition $115

APPLEBAUGH, JOHN (Thunderbird Knives) Arkansas Toothpick, 12" blade, brass hilt and butt, ebony handle $225

APPLEBAUGH, JOHN (Thunderbird Knives) Dagger, 6½" blade, brass hilt and butt, rosewood handle, no sheath $105

ARA Fighter, 5¾" blade, brass hilt, wood handle, entire knife blackened $145

ARGENTINA Gaucho, 5½" German blade, brass bolster and inlays $75

ARGENTINA Gaucho, 6" blade, silver metal handle and sheath, blade is ordinary (new) but the handle and sheath are very nice indeed $150

ATKINSON Drop point skinner, 3" blade, tapered tang, finger groove stag scales, serial #80 ..... $65

AURUM ENGRAVING Lockback, 3½" closed, nickel silver bolsters, stag scales, etched blade, leather pouch $45

AURUM ENGRAVING Lockback, 4⅝" closed, nickel silver bolsters, stag scales, etched blade, has been sharpened, laced leather belt pouch $35

AURUM ENGRAVING NRA Commemorative Bowie, 6½" etched blade, most dressed up version I have seen, no sheath, walnut chest $320

AYER Skinner, 4¼" blade, brass hilt pins, burgundy Micarta handle $85

B

BAGWELL 5½" blade, brass bolster, carved ebony handle $345

BAGWELL Bowie, 8¾" cable damascus blade, very thick brass hilt, India stag $545

BAGWELL Bowie, 9" cable damascus blade, file-worked brass hilt, India stag, blade scratched $455

BAGWELL Bowie, 9" cable damascus steel blade, brass hilt, India stag handle $475

BAGWELL Bowie, 9¼" damascus blade, brass hilt, exotic wood handle $395

BAGWELL Bowie, 9½" blade (7/16 thick at hilt), brass hilt, stag handle $495

BAGWELL Dagger, 9¼" damascus steel blade, nickel silver hilt and butt, wire-wrapped ebony handle, no sheath, zipper case, far and away the very best Bagwell I have seen $795

BAGWELL Drop point, 6¾" blade, brass hilt, stag slabs, lightly used $355

BAGWELL Hunter, 6" cable damascus blade, antique stag handle $245

BAGWELL Lockback, 3" closed, damascus blade, nickel silver bolsters, brass liners and pins, rosewood slabs, used $295

BALISONG Butterfly, 5⅛" closed, drop point blade, stainless handles, handmade $345

BAGWELL Push dagger, 3" damascus blade, oosic handle, no sheath $250

BALISONG Butterfly, 4⅜" closed, model 30, all stainless steel, sheath, new $45

BALISONG Butterfly, 4⅜" closed, all stainless steel, sheath, blade scratched $125

BALISONG Butterfly, 5" closed, stainless bolsters and liners, ivory Micarta scales, belt sheath, new $265

BALISONG Butterfly, 5" closed, bead blasted handle and blade $175

BALISONG Butterfly, 5¼" closed, Wee Hawk model, filework blade, all stainless steel, sheath $285

BALISONG Butterfly, Model 35, all stainless steel, satin finish blade $50

BALISONG Butterfly, tanto blade, 5¼" closed, all stainless steel, sheath $285

BARBEE Upswept skinner, 4" blade, brass pins, white liners, wood Micarta slabs $115

BARDSLEY Fighter, 4¼" blade, stainless hilt, rosewood scales, new $150

BAREFOOT, JOE W., Drop point, 3¼" blade, stainless bolster and hilt, exotic wood handles, nice ... $115

BAREFOOT, JOE W. Hunter, 2⅞" blade, stainless hilt and pins, Brazilian rosewood scales, tapered tang, red liners, mirror finish, new $125

BARNES Slipjoint, 2⅜" closed, brass liners and bolsters, ox horn scales, file work backspring ... $125

BARNETT Slipjoint, 3¼" closed, nickel silver bolsters, liners, ivory scales $170

BARR Bootknife, 5" double-ground blade, handrubbed nickel silver hilt, mastodon ivory $395

BARRETT Slipjoint, 3½" closed, made 1980, stainless bolster liner, exotic hardwood scales $175

BARRETT Slipjoint, 4" closed, stainless bolster and liners, stag scales $175

BARRETT Slipjoint, 4" closed, stainless bolster, liners and Pins, ebony slabs, mirror finish blade $125

BARRETT Slipjoint, 4" closed, one 154CM blade, stainless liners and bolsters, kingwood scales $140

BARRETT & CLAIR 3" damascus blade, nickel silver hilt, tang and pins, stag scales, hilt, pins and back of tang engraved $155

BAYONET Pike bayonet, 17¼" long, 4 grooves, unusual $45

BEAN, L.L. Trapper Bullet slipjoint, 4½" closed, brass bolsters, liners and inlay, wood Micarta handle, box with pouch and belt sheath, new $235

BEAN, L.L. Trapper Bullet slipjoint, 4½" closed, brass bolsters, liners and inlay, India stag scales, box with pouch and belt sheath, new $275

BEARPAW Slipjoint, 4" closed, nickel silver bolsters, pins and liners, maple scales $65

BEAVER, BUTCH Bootknife, 4" single edge blade of 440C, bronze bolsters exotic wood scales, snakeskin sheath $165

BEAVER, BUTCH Bowie, massive 12" blade, brass hilt, India stag handle, Butch's well-known high quality, no sheath $325

BEAVER, BUTCH Set of three tantos, 5¾″, 7½″ and 8¾″ blades matching handles and tsuba, very fine red velvet lined chest $795

BECK Drop point, 4″ blade, nickel silver hilt, very fine rosewood scales, #131 .... $125

BECK Drop point, 3½″ blade, stag scales, #262 $135

BECK Drop point, 3¾″ blade, nickel silver hilt, stag scales $95

BECK Drop point hunter, 2⅞″ blade, nickel silver pins, burgundy Micarta slabs, tapered tang, mirror finish blade, #670 .... $75

BECK Gentleman's hunter, 3″ blade, stainless hilt and pins, brown Micarta slabs, tapered tang, satin finish $115

BECKER Machax survival, 10″ blade, brass pins, walnut slabs, black blade, new $85

BEERS, R. RB Bootknife, 3½″ blade, nickel silver hilt, tapered tang, black liners, stag scales, new .. $155

BEERS, R. Drop point skinner, 3¾″ blade, stainless hilt, ivory Micarta handle, hollow ground blade, mirror finish, #25, new $225

BEERS, R. Tanto, 5⅜″ blade of 440C stainless steel, ironwood hilt and ivory handle, ironwood sheath $195

BEERS, RAY S. Kukri fighter, 7⅝″ blade, black Micarta scales, interesting fighter, well done $255

BENCHMARK Bootknife, 4″ blade, 2″ serrations one side, zytel handle, shoulder harness $115

BENCHMARK Rolox, 2⅞″ closed, stainless bolster and liners, ivory Micarta scales, box $275

BENCHMARK Rolox, 2⅞″ closed, stainless bolster and liners, cocobolo scales, new box $285

BENCHMARK Rolox, 3⅞″ closed, stainless bolsters and liners, India stag scales, box $275

BENCHMARK Rolox, 3⅞″ closed, stainless bolster and liners, satin finish blade, cocobolo scales, belt sheath, original box, new $225

BENCHMARK Rolox, 4″ closed, stainless bolsters and liners, inlay cocobolo scales, satin finish blade $255

BENCHMARK Rolox, 4¼″ closed, stainless bolster and liners, rosewood scales, has been sharpened and carried $165

BENCHMARK Rolox, 4⅜″ closed, stainless liners and bolsters, black Micarta scales, box $225

BENCHMARK Rolox, 4⅜″ closed, stainless bolsters and liners, ivory Micarta scales, box $265

BENCHMARK Rolox Viper, 3¾″ closed, stainless bolsters and liners, stag scales, sheath $325

BENCHMARK Side Winder, 3" closed, satin finish blade, stainless bolster and liners, stag slabs, original box, new $275

BENCHMARK Survival, 4" blade, stainless hilt, stag slabs, small crack at butt between stag and tang $115

BENCH-MADE BUSHMASTER 9¾" blade, black rubber handle, used $60

BENNETT Hunter, 5¼" blade, nickel silver, 17 handle materials $155

BENTON Bootknife, 4⅜" blade, burgundy Micarta $115

BERETTA Dagger, 3¾" blade, nickel silver hilt, rosewood scales, very nice presentation box, #156 $75

BERETTA Dagger, 5¼" blade, nickel silver hilt and butt, rosewood scales, serial #156, presentation box $125

BESIC Clip point hunter, 3⅝" blade, engraved (sculpted) stainless bolsters by Gary Blanchard, pau ferro scales, no sheath, zippered case (this maker does a really nice hand-rubbed blade) $355

BESIC Spearpoint hunter, 5⅛" blade, stainless hilt, rosewood scales (an early knife by a very talented maker, here you can see the promise of what his work has since become) $125

BIANCHI Nighthawk fighter, 6" bead blasted saw-tooth blade, brass hilt and butt compass, hollow dark green delrin handle, #1653 .... $165

BIRT Bootknife, 4⅛" blade, nickel silver bolster, zebra wood handle, early knife by one of today's top makers $175

BIRT Bowie, 6" blade, brass hilt and sheath fittings, ivory Micarta scales, early knife by great maker   30

BLACKJACK Blackmoor Dirk, 6¼" blade, black rubber handle, stainless hilt, satin finish blade, new $75

BLACKJACK Mamba, 9½" blade, as new ($170 retail new) $115

BLACKJACK Tartan Dirk, 9" blade, ($120 retail new) $95

BLACKJACK Wasp thrower ($70 retail new) $50

BOKER Two-blade senator, 4¼" closed, brass liners, fancy nickel silver bolsters, plastic scales, Prairie Schooner inlay $35

BOKER Two-blade serpentine, 4" closed, brass liners, nickel silver bolsters, plastic scales, nickel silver The Alamo inlay $40

BOKER Two-blade serpentine, 4" closed, brass liners, nickel silver bolsters, plastic scales, Buffalo Bill/Sitting Bull inlay $35

BOKER Two-blade swell-center jack, 5¼" closed, nickel silver bolsters, brass liners, wood scales, used $35

BOKER Three-blade Wharncliffe stock, 4" closed, nickel silver bolsters and liners, plastic scales, etched blade $40

BOKER Four-blade congress, 3¾" closed, brass liners, fancy nickel silver bolsters, plastic scales, Remember the Maine inlay $50

BOKER Wharncliffe whittler, 3½" closed, brass liners, nickel silver bolsters, white iced celluloid The Sternwheeler scales $55

BOKER (GERMANY) Bowie, 5" blade, brass hilt and butt, birds eye wood handle $60

BOKER Ceramic lockback, 2⅝" closed, gray titanium handle with blue engraving, ceramic blade $75

BOKER (GERMANY) Set of three pockets—one four-blade congress and two three-blade stock-named Lee, Jackson and Davis, music box chest plays Dixie $95

BOKER (GERMANY) Skinner, 5⅛" blade, aluminum hilt and butt, leather handle, #159 .... $35

BOKER (GERMANY) Skinner, 5⅛" blade, aluminum hilt and butt, leather handle $35

BOKER (GERMANY) Two-blade jack, 3" closed, nickel silver bolsters, brass liners, jigged bone scales $35

BOLTON Bootknife, 3" blade, ivory Micarta scales $125

BONE 4" blade, nickel silver hilt and butt, black Micarta and brass spacers, oosic handle $195

BONE Bird and trout, 4" blade, & brass hilt and butt, leather handle $145

BONE Bowie, 10" blade, brass hilt and butt, buffalo horn handle $325

BONE Drop point, 3" blade, brass and black Micarta bolster, brass butt, hardwood handle, SID on back of blade, no sheath $120

BONE Drop point, 4½" blade, brass hilt and pins, rosewood scales $135

BONE Hunter, 5" blade, brass hilt and butt, rosewood handle $145

BONE Hunter, 5" blade, brass hilt and butt cap, rosewood handle $125

BONE Model J lockback, 5" blade, brass bolsters and liners, rosewood handle, #1237, belt pouch .. $295

BONE Skinner, 4″ blade, brass hilt and butt, black Micarta spacers, rosewood finger groove handle, #233 .... $165

BONE Skinner, 4¼″ blade, brass hilt and butt, ebony handle $145

BONE Skinner, 4½″ blade, stainless hilt, butt and spacers, black spacers, rose wood handle, blade marked U 290, used, ... $135

BONSA Cigar shaped fruit tester, 3½″ closed, nickel silver bolsters, brass liners, nickel silver inlay, jigged bone scales $55

BOOTH, LEW Hunter, 3⅞″ blade, engraved, nickel silver hilt, rosewood scales $155

BOOTH, LEW 4⅞″ blade, integral hilt, very tapered tang, red liners, black Micarta handle $195

BOOTH, LEW Drop point, 3⅞″ blade, brass inlaid tang, stainless hilt and pins, black Micarta scales, Booth worked in the late 60s and early 70s $155

BOOTH, LEW Drop point, 4″ blade, flatground brass hilt, black Micarta scales $155

BOOTH, LEW Hunter, 5⅞″ blade, integral hilt, black Micarta scales $220

BOWEN All steel belt buckle knife, 2⅝″ blade $25

BOWEN All steel thrower, 5½″ blade $35

BOWEN Lockback, 3½″ closed, stainless steel bolsters and liners, black Micarta scales, etched blade $60

BOWEN Lockback, 4½″, nickel silver bolsters, brass liners, stag scales, sharpened, not carried $45

BOWEN Model 12 fighter, 8½″ clip point blade, brass pins, wood Micarta handle $65

BOWER IMP CO. (SOLINGEN) Bowie, 6⅛″ blade, brass hilt, aluminum butt, wood handle, used $40

BOYE Hunter, 4⅛″ blade, finger groove hilt, brass inlay, cocobolo handle, etched hollow ground blade, unused $185

BOYE Skinner, 3½″ blade, brass hilt, rosewood scales, blade etched with lion from Oz $165

BOYE Skinner, 4″ blade with nicely etched fox as robin hood, brass hilt, rosewood scales $165

BRIDGEPORT HARDWARE MFG. CORP. Boy Scout belt ax, 13¼″ long with 3¼″ cutting edge, forged one piece handle and head, wood scales applied with rivets, one cracked, no sheath $140

BRIDWELL 3¾″ blade, stainless hilt and pins, tapered tang, black liners, ivory Micarta slabs, mirror finish $225

BRIDWELL Drop point, 4″ blade, fileworked nickel silver hilt, fileworked cracked ivory scales with scrimmed drinking leopards good enough to justify keeping these handles $215

BRIDWELL Frontlock, 4¾″ blade, stainless steel liners and bolsters, ironwood scales $125

BRIDWELL Hunter, 3½″ blade, stainless steel hilt and pins, ivory, very nice little hunter $335

BRITTON Bootknife, 3½″ blade, nickel silver butt, ivory Micarta scales, satin finish $140

BRITTON Bootknife, 4⅛″ single-edge parkerized blade, black Micarta scales $130

BRITTON, TIM Skean dhu, 3½″ blade, stainless steel bolster and butt, very fine pearl scales, no sheath, walnut presentation box $265

BROOKS Clip point hunter, 3⅛″ blade, forged 0-1 stainless hilt and butt cap, exotic wood handle .. $90

BROOKS, S.R. Bowie, beautiful damascus 8″ blade, iron hilt and bolsters, India stag scales, sheath with stud $375

BROOKS, S.R. Drop point hunter, 5″ damascus steel blade, brass hilt pins, fancy walnut $275

BROOKS, S.R. Fighter, very fine damascus steel 6″ blade, damascus steel hilt, brass pins, rosewood scales, waist band sheath with stud $365

BROOKS, S.R. Tanto, 6″ handsome damascus steel blade, mortise tang, exotic wood handle, very nice $365

BROOKS, STEVE Bowie, 8¼″ fine damascus steel blade, damascus hilt, very fancy ironwood handle $635

BROWNE, R.C. Hunter, 4⅛″ blade, stainless hilt, cocobolo handle $220

BROWN & PHARR Two-blade reverse congress, 3⅜″ closed, nickel silver bolsters, brass liners, screwed not pinned rosewood scales $225

BROWNING Lockback, 4″ closed, brass frame, jade inlays, serial #76, walnut box $175

BROWNING Lockback, Model #3018F1, 4¼″ closed, brass bolsters, caps and liners, exotic wood scales, leather belt pouch $25

BROWNING Lockback, 4¼″ closed, brass bolsters and liners, stag scales, damascus blade, box $355

BROWNING (GERMANY) Lockback, 4¼″ closed, brass bolsters and liners, wood scales, leather belt sheath $115

BROWNING (GERMANY) Three-blade congress, 3¼" closed, brass liners, nickel silver bolsters, rosewood scales, original box, mint $115

BROWNING (JAPAN) Three-blade lockback, Model 504, 4½" closed, deer on blade, brass bolsters, liners and pins, stag slabs, sharpened, leather sheath $40

BROWNING (USA) Lockback, 4⅛" closed, brass frames, wood Micarta scales, leather belt pouch, box $55

BROWNING (USA) Lockback, 4⅞" closed, brass frames, wood Micarta scales $85

BRUCKMANN Two-blade, 3½" closed, corkscrew, nickel silver bolsters, brass liners, jacaranda wood handle, at least 50 years old, mint $25

BRUCKMANN Two-blade, 3½" closed, cattle horn scales, mint $25

BRUCKMANN Two-blade jack, 3 5/16" closed, corkscrew, brass liners, nickel silver bolsters, cattle horn scales $45

BRUCKMANN Two-blade senator, 3" closed, milled brass liners, nickel silver tips, stag scales $175

BRUCKMANN Two-blade senator, 3¼" closed, scissors, corkscrew, nickel silver bolsters and liners, cattle horn handles $120

BRUCKMANN Two-blade senator, 3 9/16" closed, shadow pattern Brass liners, cattle horn scales $20

BRUCKMANN Three-blade sleeveboard whittler, 3¼" closed, milled brass liners, nickel silver bolsters, inlay cattle horn scales, very nice, very rare $185

BRUCKMANN Four-blade pen, 2⅞" closed, nickel silver bolsters, milled brass liners, rare European stag scales, mint $145

BUCK Model 102, 4" blade, brass hilt, butt cocobolo handle, special limited edition $65

BUCK 103 skinner, 4" blade, aluminum hilt and butt, black Micarta scales, new $25

BUCK Model 112 lockback, 4¼" closed, brass frames, rosewood scales, pouch $35

BUCK Model 119 Special, 6" bowie blade, aluminum hilt and butt, black handle $40

BUCK Model 119 Special, 6" 425M 58/60 R, bowie blade, brass hilt and butt, mesquite wood handle, mirror polish finish, new, letter of authenticity from Buck $150

BUCK LT Model 185 Buckmaster, 7⅛" blade, black-coated handle with finger grooves, dull finish saw-tooth blade, molded plastic sheath, original box $75

BUCK Model 317 two-blade swell center jack, 5¼″ closed, brass liners, nickel silver bolsters and inlay, delrin scales, carried and used, black belt sheath $25

BUCK Model 426 Bucklite lockback, 5″ closed, lightweight brown zytel handle $25

BUCK Custom, 6″ blade ground like old Draper, stainless steel bolster, black wood Micarta, no sheath $125

BUCK Model 500 Colt Custom lockback, 4¼″ closed, gold and black blade etched Colt Firearms, stainless bolster and liners, wood Micarta slabs, Colt brass inlay, #276, presentation wood case $135

BUCK Model 506 lockback, 2⅞″ closed, stainless bolsters and liners, ivory slabs, deer scrimshaw, #03 .... $100

BUCK Custom 100th Anniversary, 6⅝″ dagger blade, nickel silver hilt and inlay, stag scales, gold etched blade, wood display box, no sheath $230

BUCK Custom bowie, 6″ blade, aluminum hilt and butt, stag handle, unused $75

BUCK Custom bowie, 10″ gold etched blade, brass lugged hilt, wood Micarta, no sheath, fine pine box lined with blue velvet, #119 of 4500 .... $255

BUCK Custom bowie, 10¼″ blade, brass hilt and pins, wood grain slabs, mirror finish blade, wood display plaque, original box, new, no sheath $155

BUCK Custom clip point hunter, 5½″ blade, brass hilt, exotic wood scales $125

BUCK Custom Eagle Model by Navajo Artist Dave Yellowhorse, brass bolster and inlay, turquoise and red spacers, wood slabs, satin finish blade, presentation box $265

BUCK Custom lockback, 4¼″ closed, stainless steel frames, India stag scales, pouch $100

BUCK Custom Yellowhorse Model by Navajo Artist Dave Yellowhorse, brass bolsters and inlay, red, turquoise inlays with wood slabs, satin finish, presentation box $225

BUCK American's Favorite inlay, satin finish blade, original box, new $25

BUCK BuckMaster, 7½″ saw tooth blade, steel hilt and butt cap, hollow handle, compass, never used $95

BUCK BuckMaster, 7½″ blade, steel hilt and but cap, hollow steel handle $95

BUCK Hatchet, black Micarta handle with finger grooves, stainless pins, used, sheath $50

BUCK Hunters ax, 10½″ overall length, wood scales, satin finish blade, sheath, original box, new ... $45

BUCK Hunters ax, 10½" overall, 2½" cutting edge, wood Micarta handles, never used $50

BUCK Lockback, 4¼" closed, brass liners and bolsters, black and white Micarta handle, new $50

BUCK Original Kalinga, 5" blade, Brass hilt Black Micarta scales, presentation box, very hard to find $195

BUCK Skinner, 4⅛" blade, aluminum hilt and butt, black Micarta handle, used $25

BUCK Statue of Liberty lockback 1886-1986, 3⅞" closed, etched blade, stainless scales protected by clear plastic, Statue of Liberty Banner handle medallion, authentic materials from the Statue of Liberty-Ellis Island National Monument, box $45

BUCK Statue of Liberty Commemorative, 4⅜" closed, oak scales from Ellis Island, copper inlay from the statue, wood display plaque $115

BUCK Yellowhorse Indian Jewelry lockback, 4¼" closed, Brass, turquoise and wood handle, presentation box, mint $195

BUCK Yellowhorse Maverick slipjoint, 3½" closed, brass turquoise, silver and wood scales, box $130

BUCK (USA) Lockback, 4¼" closed, brass bolsters, caps and liners, walnut scales $45

BUD Drop point, 2½" blade, stainless hilt, matched stag scales $65

BULLDOG Two-blade sleeveboard jack, 4¼" closed, brass liners, nickel silver bolsters and inlay, black and green celluloid scales $65

BULLDOG Two-blade Wharncliffe, 4" closed, brass liners, nickel silver bolster and inlay, celluloid scales, etched blade $70

BUND Camp set (knife, fork, spoon and opener), 7½", all stainless steel, sheath $50

BURDEKIN Sheffield bowie, 5⅞" blade, nickel silver hilt, inlay, stag scales, sheath has lost tip, well used and very old $100

BURTON 4⅛" blade, brass hilt, brown and tan Micarta scales $75

BURTON 4¾" blade, brass hilt, fancy walnut scales $75

BURTON Hunter, 5½" blade, nickel silver hilt, wood Micarta slabs, filework blade back, mirror finish $75

BUSTER, FRANK One-blade canoe, 3¾" closed, brass liners, nickel silver bolsters, green delrin scales, gold Fight'n Rooster on handle $55

BUSTER, FRANK One-blade canoe, 3¾" closed, brass liners, nickel silver bolsters and pins, red celluloid or delrin slabs, gold Fight'n Rooster on handle ... $65

BUSTER, FRANK One-blade jack, 3⅝" closed, brass liners, yellow scales, inlay $45

BUSTER, FRANK One-blade jack, 5" closed, nickel silver bolsters and inlay, brass liners, yellow celluloid scales, etched blade $70

BUSTER, FRANK One-blade sleeveboard jack, 3" closed, nickel silver bolsters, brass liners, pearl scales, etched Gem Miner 1982 Franklin NC, #160 of 300, new $55

BUSTER, FRANK One-blade slipjoint, 5" closed, nickel silver bolsters and inlay, brass liner, bone scales, etched blade $50

BUSTER, FRANK One-blade slipjoint, 5" closed, nickel silver bolsters and inlay, brass liners, black and gray celluloid scales, etched blade $60

BUSTER, FRANK Two-blade, 3⅝" closed, nickel silver bolsters and pins, brass liners, cattle horn scales, gold etched Physician's Knife $65

BUSTER, FRANK Two-blade barlow, 3⅝" closed, nickel silver bolster, brass liners, pearl scales, etched International Fight'n Rooster 1981, #317 of 600,

BUSTER, FRANK Two-blade canoe, 3⅝" closed, brass liners, nickel silver bolsters, cattle horn scales, Merry Christmas 1985 etched Fight'n Rooster $55

BUSTER, FRANK Two-blade canoe, 3⅝" closed, brass liners, nickel silver bolster and pins, black and white stripped celluloid scales, etched blade. $65

BUSTER, FRANK Two-blade canoe, 3⅝" closed, engraved nickel silver bolsters, brass liners, jigged bone scales, etched $55

BUSTER, FRANK Two-blade canoe, 3¾" closed, brass liners, nickel silver bolsters, pins and inlay, black delrin scales, etched blade Fight'n Rooster. $65

BUSTER, FRANK Two-blade congress, 3¾" closed, nickel silver bolsters, brass liners, pearl scales, blade etched Middle Tennessee Knife Collectors 1982, #349 of 400, new $70

new **$95**

BUSTER, FRANK Two-blade etched Gem Capital Knife Club 1983, 3 ¾" closed, nickel silver bolsters and spacer, brass liners, pearl scales, #000 of 300, new $75

BUSTER, FRANK Two-blade even-end pen, 3½″ closed, brass liners, nickel silver pins and inlay, black, gold and white celluloid scales, etched blade $45
BUSTER, FRANK Two-blade gunstock, 3½″ closed, nickel silver bolsters, brass liners, amber scales, etched Fight'n Rooster $45
BUSTER, FRANK Two-blade jack, 3″ closed, nickel silver bolsters and inlay, brass liners, orange and black celluloid scales, etched $40
BUSTER, FRANK Two-blade jack, 4⅛″ closed, nickel silver inlay, bolsters and pins, brass liners, iced blue celluloid scales, Tennessee Homecoming '86 etched gold and red, #125 of 200 .... $65
BUSTER, FRANK Two-blade jack, 5″ closed, nickel silver bolsters and inlay, brass liners, multi-color metallic celluloid scales, etched 70
BUSTER, FRANK Two-blade muskrat, 4″ closed, nickel silver bolsters and inlay, brass liners, royal blue and white celluloid scales, etched $45
BUSTER, FRANK Two-blade leg-knife jack, 3¼″ closed, nickel silver inlay, brass liners green and white scales, etched blade $35
BUSTER, FRANK Two-blade serpentine jack, 3⅝″ closed, nickel silver bolsters, inlay, pins and liners, bone scales, etched blade $50
BUSTER, FRANK Two-blade trapper jack, 4⅛″ closed, nickel silver bolsters and inlay, brass liners, stag scales, etched blade $60
BUSTER, FRANK Two-blade serpentine, 4″ closed, nickel silver bolsters and inlay, brass liners, jigged bone scales, etched blade $40
BUSTER, FRANK Two-blade serpentine, 4″ closed, nickel silver bolsters, inlay and pins, brass liners, orange and black celluloid scales, etched blade $45
BUSTER, FRANK Three-blade premium stock, 3⅝″ closed, brass liners, nickel silver bolsters and inlay, multi-color celluloid scales, etched blade $95
BUSTER, FRANK Three-blade stock, 3¾″ closed, nickel silver inlay and pins, brass liners, red, blue old and green metallic celluloid scales, etched blade $45
BUSTER, FRANK Three-blade congress whittler, 4″ closed, nickel silver bolsters and inlay, brass liners, cattle horn scales, gold etched Fight'n Rooster $85
BUSTER, FRANK Three-blade senator, 3½″ closed, nickel silver bolsters and inlay, brass liners, black, blue and gray celluloid scales, gold etched 1985 Cattleman $75

BUSTER, FRANK Three-blade premium stock, 3⅞" closed, nickel silver bolsters and inlay, brass liners, gray iced celluloid scales, gold etched 1986 Rough Cut $70

BUSTER, FRANK Three-blade stock, 3¾" closed, nickel silver bolsters and inlay, brass liners, bone scales, etched blade $65

BUSTER, FRANK Three-blade stock serpentine, 3¾" closed, nickel silver bolsters and pins, brass liners, red, gold and blue celluloid scales, etched nude woman $65

BUSTER, FRANK Three-blade Wharncliffe, 3⅞" closed, nickel silver bolsters and inlay, brass liners, multi-color celluloid scales, etched $85

BUSTER, FRANK Four-blade canoe, 3⅝" closed, nickel silver bolsters and inlay, brass liners, cattle horn scales, gold etched Fight'n Rooster $95

BUSTER, FRANK 12-blade, 3⅝" closed, nickel silver bolsters and inlay, brass liners, stag slabs, etched $155

BUSTER, FRANK 12-blade congress, 3⅝" closed, nickel silver bolsters, brass liners, mother of pearl scales, Fight'n Rooster 1985, #212 of 600. .... $195

BUSTER, FRANK 3⅞" closed, nickel silver bolsters, brass liners, pearl scales, blade etched Middle Tennessee 1981 Knife Collectors, #327 of 400, new ... $85

BUSTER, FRANK Cajun Queen toothpick, 5⅛" closed, ornate nickel silver bolsters and inlay, brass liners, jigged bone scales, 1 of 600, serial #212 $75

BUSTER, FRANK Californian midlock, 4½" closed, gold etched blade, brass liners, nickel silver bolsters, stag handle $95

BUSTER, FRANK Coal Digger Special 1983 three-blade stock, 3¾" closed, nickel silver bolsters and inlay, brass liners, black and white celluloid scales, gold etched blade, #490 of 1000 .... $55

BUSTER, FRANK Copperhead two-blade jack, 3¾" closed, nickel silver bolsters and inlay, brass liners, stag scales, etched $75

BUSTER, FRANK Lockback, 4⅜" closed, brass liners, nickel silver bolsters and inlay, stag slabs, etched Old Dominion 1988 #172 of 200, Knife Collectors Assn. $75

BUSTER, FRANK Lockback whittler, 3⅞" closed, nickel silver bolsters, inlay and pins, brass liners, cattle horn scales $125

BUSTER, FRANK New Orleans toothpick, 5⅛" closed, ornate nickel silver bolsters and inlay, stag scales, 1 of 600, serial #212 .... $95

BUSTER, FRANK Serpentine jack, 3⅜" closed, nickel silver inlay, brass liners, cattle horn scales, etched $35

BUSTER, FRANK Skid Row 1987 two-blade, 4⅛" closed, nickel silver inlay and pins, brass liners, imitation tortoise shell scales, etched blade, #11 of 400 .... $55

BUSTER, FRANK Sleeveboard whittler, 3⅝" closed, nickel silver bolsters, brass liners, pearl scales, blade etched Williamson County 1981, #40 of 80, new $85

BUSTER, FRANK Slipjoint, 5" closed, nickel silver bolsters, liners and spacer, pearl handle, etched Middle Tennessee Knife Collectors 1980, #16 of 400 .... $70

BUSTER, FRANK whittler, midlock main blade, 3⅞" closed, nickel silver bolsters, brass liners, pearl scales, main blade gold plated, etched Fightin' Rooster, new $115

C

C.C.C. Barlow, 3¼" closed, iron bolsters and liners, bone scales $75

C.I. Butterfly, 5" closed, 440C stainless drop point blade, brass liners $20

CALDWELL Bowie, 5", nickel silver hilt and butt, India stag handle, very nice little bowie in pocket or waistband sheath $225

CAM-II Lockback with guthook, 4¼" closed, nickel silver liners and bolsters, black Micarta scales, satin finish blade, belt sheath, new $30

CAM-III (JAPAN) Lockback physicians, 4⅛" closed, nickel silver bolsters and butt, brass liners, walnut scales $35

CAM-III (JAPAN) Phantom lockback, 4½" closed, nickel silver bolsters, caps and liners, pearl and nickel silver scales $65

CAMPBELL, R.C. Slipjoint, 3½" closed, stainless liners and bolsters, crushed Micarta scales, needs adjusting by maker (joint too tight, blade tip a touch too long), seems very early knife by talented maker $80

CAMILLUS 4½″ blade, brass hilt, aluminum butt, leather handle, used $20

CAMILLUS American Wildlife Series two-blade swell center jack, 4½″ closed, brass liners, nickel silver bolsters, deer inlay plastic handles, sharpening rod, original box $55

CAMILLUS Cattle, 4⅛″, nickel silver bolsters, brass liners, US SIGNAL CORP inlay, ebony scales (small chip out of one side), very good condition ... $95

CAMILLUS Linerlock fish, 5″ blade, iron liners, bolsters and caps, used, old, rough black condition but not worn $30

CAMILLUS Model #10, two-blade equal-end jack, 3⅝″ closed, brass liners, nickel silver bolsters, jigged bone scales $20

CAMILLUS Model #12 two-blade sleeveboard jack, 3½″ closed, brass liners, nickel silver bolsters, jigged bone scales, made in 50s $110

CARGILL 2⅝″ blade, brass pins, nickel silver hilt, burgundy Micarta slabs, satin finish $110

CARGILL Drop point skinner, 3¾″ blade, engraved nickel silver hilt, satin finish blade, stag slabs $155

CARTER, FRED Bootknife, 4″ 440C blade, nickel silver hilt, pins and file worked liners, stag ivory scales, prototype #1, early Fred Carter $255

CARTER, FRED Drop point, 3¾″ 0-1 hollow-ground blade, engraved brass bolsters, cocobolo scales, no sheath, zippered pouch $395

CARTER Drop point, 3¾″ 0-1 flat ground blade, brass bolsters, stag scales, no sheath, zippered case $385

CARTER, FRED Drop point, 3¾″ 0-1 hollow ground blade, brass bolsters, stag scales, no sheath, zippered case $385

CARTER, FRED Drop point hunter, 3¼″ blade, integral hilt and butt, ironwood scales, early Carter showing clearly the maker he would become, unmarked $195

CARTER, FRED Fighter, 6¾″ blade, bead blasted blade, bolster and butt, black Micarta slabs, no sheath $585

CARTER, FRED Spear point fighter, 4¾″ blade, stainless bolster and pins, tapered tang, burgundy liners, black Micarta slabs, new $385

CASE 1 DOT Model #12031L two-blade electrician, 3¾″ closed, spear point and combination screwdriver and wire stripper, nickel silver bolsters and inlay, brass liners, walnut scales $30

CASE 5 DOT five-blade stock, 4" closed, nickel silver bolsters, brass liners $115

CASE 7 DOT Shark Tooth Model 7197L SSP, 5" closed, brass frames, pacawood inserts, pouch, new $75

CASE 8 DOT Model P62-4½ bootknife, 4½" satin-finish blade, stainless hilt and butt, black Micarta slabs, box, new $70

CASE 8 DOT hawk-billed pruner, 4" closed, nickel silver bolsters, brass liners, walnut scales ... $30

CASE 9 DOT Shark tooth lockback, 5" closed, brass frame, stag scales, pouch, box, new $85

CASE Bradford Centennial, 3⅛" blade, steel hilt and aluminum butt, stag scales $55

CASE 4 DOT Sod Buster, 4¾" closed, brass liners and pins, black plastic scales $20

CASE 1 DOT Bradford Centennial Model #5275SP two-blade serpentine, 4½" closed, nickel silver bolsters and inlay, brass liners, stag scales $45

CASE 1 DOT Bradford Centennial Model # 5292 SSP two-blade serpentine, 3⅞" closed, nickel silver bolsters and inlay, brass liners, stag scales $45

CASE 1 DOT Bradford Centennial, Model #5207SP SSP two-blade trapper, 3½" closed, nickel silver bolsters and inlay, brass liners, stag scales .. $45

CASE 1 DOT jack, 4⅛" closed, nickel silver bolsters and caps, brass liners, clear plastic over bathing beauty photo, serial #5664 .... $45

CASE XX USA DOT stainless sleeve board pen, 3¼" closed, nickel silver bolsters and liners, pearl scales, lightly used $45

CASE 2 DOT Hammerhead lockback, 4¾" closed, brass frames, pacawood handles $55

CASE Two-blade barlow clip and pen, 3⅜" closed, nickel silver bolsters, brass liners, stag scales, part of two-knife set #1139 .... $45

CASE Two-blade barlow 8 DOT three-knife set, 3⅜" closed, nickel silver bolsters, brass liners, stag scales, serial #4306, wood display box $225

CASE Two-blade razor barlow, 3⅜" closed, nickel silver bolsters, brass liners, stag scales, part of two-knife set #1139 .... $55

CASE Two-blade gunstock jack, 3" closed, brass liners, nickel silver bolsters and caps, green jigged bone scales, Case inlay $50

CASE Two-blade jack, 4" closed, brass liners, nickel silver bolsters, jigged bone scales, Indians in boat etched on blade by Shaw-Liebowitz $175

CASE Two-blade serpentine jack 2⅞" closed, nickel silver bolsters and inlay, brass liners, maple scales $45

CASE Two-blade swell center jack, 5¼" closed, nickel silver bolsters, brass liners, jigged bone scales, pouch $55

CASE Two-blade trapper, 4⅛" closed, nickel silver bolsters, stag scales, carried, one blade used $35

CASE 3⅝" blade, stainless hilt, aluminum butt, stag scales, 50s or 60s period, mint $75

CASE 5⅛" blade, steel hilt, aluminum butt, stag scales $45

CASE 75th Anniversary round end stock, 3⅝" closed, nickel silver bolsters, brass liners, stag scales $45

CASE Bicentennial The American Spirit, 5¼" closed, engraved, nickel silver bolsters, brass liners, stag scales $85

CASE Bradford Centennial, 3¼" blade, stainless hilt, aluminum butt, stag scales $55

CASE Bradford Centennial, Model #5249 SSP 1 DOT two-blade jack, 3⅞" closed, nickel silver bolsters and inlay, brass liners, stag scales $45

CASE Bradford Centennial Model #5318HP SSP 1 DOT stock, 3½" closed, nickel silver bolsters and inlay, brass liners stag scales, ... $65

CASE Bradford Centennial Model #52027 SSP 1 DOT two-blade jack, 2⅞" closed, nickel silver bolsters and inlay, brass liners, stag scales $40

CASE Bradford Centennial, 4¼" blade, steel hilt, aluminum butt, stag scales $45

CASE Bradford Centennial, 5" blade aluminum butt, steel hilt, stag scales $55

CASE Buffalo clasp, 5½" closed, 10 DOT, nickel silver bolsters and caps, brass liners, pacawood scales, box, mint $155

CASE Bulldog clasp, 5½" closed, nickel silver bolsters, caps and inlay, brass liners, stag scales, wood display box, minor blade pitting $155

CASE Circle C Tested XX electrician's two-blade spear point combined screwdriver and wire stripper, government spec. #TL-29, 3¾" closed, nickel silver bolsters and liners, rosewood scales, very fine $100

CASE Daddy barlow drop point, No. 6143, 5" closed, iron bolsters, liners, sawed bone scales $25

CASE Dagger, 4½" blade, nickel silver hilt, wood Micarta handle $35

CASE 1988 Fox Hunter serpentine trapper two-knife set, 2⅞" and 4½" closed, nickel silver bolsters and caps, brass liners, stag scales, display box, serial #401 .... $85

CASE Eight-knife Collectors Set, different sizes and kinds, all 3 DOT, nickel silver bolsters and inlays, brass liners, stag handles and blue scroll etched blades, display box $355

CASE Kentucky Bicentennial slipjoint, 3½" closed, green plastic scales, box, mint $40

CASE Mako Model #P159 LSSP lockback, 4¼" closed, brass frames, wood Micarta scales, leather belt pouch $40

CASE Moby Dick clasp, 5¼" closed, nickel silver bolsters, engraved, brass liners, delrin whalebone scales, scrimmed whaling scene one side .. $125

CASE Model #0L2781 DOT two-blade pen, 3" closed, cast sterling silver scales (skaters one side, skiers and Lake Placid 1980 on the other), very nice little knife, box, serial #1833 .... $200

CASE Remember The Alamo Commemorative bowie, 9⅜" blade, nickel silver hilt and pins, red Micarta spacer, walnut handles, oak chest, no sheath $165

CASE Set of three 75th Anniversaries, glass-topped wood case $300

CASE Shark Tooth lockback Model #P197 L SSP, 5" closed, brass frames, wood Micarta scales, leather belt pouch $45

CASE Sidewinder, 5⅛" closed, inlay lock release, nickel silver bolsters, brass liners wood Micarta scales $75

CASE Skinner, 5" blade, brass hilt and butt, stag handle $40

CASE Slipjoint single-blade jack, delrin bone scales, nickel silver bolsters, brass liners $15

CASE Sleeveboard jack, 5⅜" closed, nickel silver bolster, brass liners and inlay, jigged light bone scales, blade etched Hailey's Comet 1986, #0984, box, new $75

CASE Smokey Mountain Trapper Set three heavy trappers, 4⅛" closed, nickel silver bolsters, caps and inlay, brass liners, two have jigged bone scales, one yellow plastic, serial #235, display box $70

CASE Tested XX two-blade Office Knife, 3⅞" closed, brass liners, celluloid ivory scales, mint, Case authenticity letter $235

CASE Texas Longhorn two-blade, 4½″ closed, nickel silver bolsters, brass liners, ivory Micarta scales, leather belt pouch, box $35

CASE USA lockback, 4¼″ closed, brass bolsters, caps, pins and liners, wood Micarta scales, Mako shark etched blade $65

CASE USA Stock, 3⅝″ closed, shadow pattern, nickel silver liners, yellow handles $95

CASE USA Trapper, 4⅛″ closed, nickel silver bolsters caps brass liners jigged bone $95

CASE West Virginia Bear Ltd. Edition 3 DOT clasp, 5¼″ closed, nickel silver bolsters and inlay, brass liners, stag scales, serial #WV205, box, 1 of 425 . . . . $125

CASE XX No DOT USA Model 6214 two-blade sleeveboard jack, nickel silver bolsters, brass liners, jigged bone scales, used $35

CASE XX No DOT stainless USA premium stock, 3⅞″ closed, nickel silver bolsters and inlay, brass liners, stag scales $95

CASE XX 2 DOT Model 5275SP two-blade serpentine, 4¼″ closed nickel silver bolsters, brass liners, second-cut stag scales $45

CASE XX 3 DOT USA two-blade canoe, 4¼″ closed, nickel silver bolsters and inlay, red jigged bone scales, blade etched red, white and blue These Colors Don't Run, #392, box, new $40

CASE XX 4 DOT Razor Edge one-blade clasp, 5½″ closed, nickel silver bolsters and inlay, brass liners, stag slabs, etched blade $75

CASE XX 4 DOT USA two-blade swell center jack, 5¼″ closed, nickel silver bolsters and inlay, brass liners, jigged wood scales, used $40

CASE XX 6 DOT Model 33092 three-blade stockman, 4″ closed, nickel silver inlay, pins and liners, yellow delrin scales, small crack both sides at pin . . . $35

CASE XX 6 DOT whittler, 3⅞″ closed, nickel silver bolsters, jigged bone scales, used $40

CASE XX 8 DOT USA Model 61093 toothpick, 5″ closed, nickel silver bolsters and inlay, jigged bone scales, shows handling, not used or sharpened $75

CASE XX 10 DOT USA 6265 SAB two-blade swell center, 5¼″ closed, brass liners, stainless bolsters and inlay, jigged pacawood slabs, belt sheath used $75

CASE XX 10 DOT USA Model 62009R two-blade barlow, 3⅜" closed, nickel silver bolsters, brass liners, red bone scales $35

CASE XX, 4¼" blade, steel hilt, aluminum butt, stag scales, etched blade $50

CASE XX 1985 Gun Boat three-knife set (USS Constitution, USS Missouri, Monitor and Merrimac), 4¼" closed, nickel silver bolsters, brass liners, stag scales, serial #1990, wood presentation box $225

CASE XX Hunter, 5¼" satin-finish blade, brass hilt and butt, stag handle, new $55

CASE XX Bradford Centennial, 5⅛" blade, steel hilt, aluminum butt and cap, stag handle $45

CASE XX Bradford Centennial #523-5, 5" blade, aluminum butt, steel hilt, stag scales. $50

CASE XX Bulldog slipjoint, 5⅝" closed, nickel silver bolsters, brass liners, stag scales, box $255

CASE XX Folding machete, 11¼" closed, 10" blade, 5½" handle, steel bolsters and guard, black, bakelite handles, linerlock no sheath or blade guard, circa WW II, hard to find $105

CASE XX Model #6165 SAB clasp, 5¼" closed, nickel silver bolsters and inlay, brass liners jigged bone scales $155

CASE XX Model #61048 single-blade jack, 4" closed, nickel silver bolsters, brass liners, jigged bone scales, blade 40% worn away $25

CASE XX Model #61048 single-blade jack, 4" closed, nickel silver bolsters, brass liners, jigged bone scales, mint $95

CASE XX Model #62024 two-blade jack, 3½" closed, nickel silver bolsters, brass liners, jigged bone scales, mint $65

CASE XX Two-blade clasp, 5¼" closed, nickel silver bolsters, caps and inlay, brass liners, stag scales, used and sharpened, good condition $85

CASE XX Two-blade clasp, 5¼" closed, nickel silver bolsters, caps and inlay, brass liners, jigged bone scales, very fine $125

CASE XX Two-blade elephant's toe nail, 4⅜" closed, brass pins, nickel silver bolsters, jigged pacawood scales, unused $125

CASE XX Two-blade jack Model #6294, 4¼" closed, nickel silver bolsters and inlay, brass liners, jigged bone scales, used, excellent $65

CASE XX Two-blade pen, 2¾" closed, stainless liners and ring, pearl scales, new $45

CASE XX Two-blade and nail file lobster, 3⅛" closed, toledo scales $50

CASE XX USA hunter, 4¼" etched blade, stainless hilt and butt, stag slabs $40

CASE XX USA Model #087HE three-blade Wharncliffe cattleman, 3¼" closed, nickel silver bolsters, inlay and liners, smooth black scales, lightly used, light pitting $55

CASE XX USA Model #5299.5 regular jack, 4⅛" closed, nickel silver bolsters, caps and inlay, brass liners, stag scales $85

CASE XX USA Model #11031 SH 3 DOT pruner, 3¾" closed, nickel silver bolsters and inlay, brass liners, walnut scales $30

CASE XX USA Model #33044 stock, 3¼" closed, nickel silver rivets, inlay and liners, yellow scales, shadow pattern $55

CASE XX Model #61093 Texas Toothpick, 5" closed, nickel silver bolsters and inlay, brass liners, jigged bone scales, used, excellent $85

CASTLE KNIFE CO. (ENGLAND) Fairbairn-Sykes Commando, 6⅞" dagger blade signed Fairbairn, brass S hilt, knurled brass handle, no sheath, limited edition $145

CATTARAUGUS 6" stainless blade, hard rubber handle, Case sheath, made in 1930s or 40s .. $40

CATTARAUGUS Combat WW II, 6" blade, iron hilt and butt, leather handle, no sheath, very rough $25

CATTARAUGUS Combat 6" blade, circa WW II plexiglass handle with aluminum hilt and butt spacer, mint blade, documented WW II history would double or treble value $135

CATTARAUGUS Combat Model 225Q, 6" blade, steel hilt and butt, leather handle, best WW II combat knife, hard to find as most have been used up as hunting and work knives over the last 45 years $55

CATTARAUGUS Folding hunter, 4½" closed, split bolsterlock, engraved bolster, jigged bone scales, etched gold deer on blade, premier $225

CATTARAUGUS Hunter, 4⅝" blade, nickel silver hilt, aluminum butt, ebony handle, great shape $85

CATTARAUGUS Lockback barlow CM-10 #1151, 3¼" closed, brass liners, stainless bolsters, cartridge inlay, jigged bone scales $45

CATTARAUGUS Split-bolsterlock jack CM-12, 3″ closed, nickel silver bolster liners, jigged bone scales $30

CATTARAUGUS (USA) Folding machete, 9½″ blade, steel bolsters and linerlock, black slabs, used $125

CENTOFANTE, FRANK Bootknife, 4″ blade, nickel silver hilt and pins, burgundy Micarta handle $185

CENTOFANTE, FRANK Bootknife, 4⅛″ blade (small nicks), brass hilt, cocobolo handles, early work by one of today's master pocket knife makers ... $95

CENTOFANTE, FRANK Drop point, 4″ blade, nickel silver hilt and butt, wood Micarta handle ... $145

CENTOFANTE, FRANK Drop point hunter, 4″ blade, nickel silver hilt and pins, ivory handle, done in the Sigman style, no sheath, very nice $375

CENTOFANTE, FRANK Folding Boot side tail-lock, 4½″ closed, nickel silver frames, abalone inlays, serial #27 .... $785

CENTOFANTE, FRANK Gunstock jack, 3⅝ closed, brass liners, nickel silver bolsters, black Micarta scales, serial #3 .... $155

CENTOFANTE, FRANK Hunter, 3¼″ blade, burgundy Micarta scales, early $125

CENTOFANTE, FRANK Hunter, 4″ straight blade, nickel silver hilt and pins, Micarta handle ... $165

CENTOFANTE, FRANK Hunter, 4⅛″ straight blade, nickel silver hilt, burgundy Micarta scales .. $145

CENTOFANTE, FRANK Lockback, 3½″ closed, nickel silver caps and bolster liners, buffalo horn handles, Serial # 2, (not the second lockback Frank made but the second of this style, made perhaps 2 years after his first folder) $335

CENTOFANTE, FRANK Lockback 3¾″ closed, nickel silver bolsters and liners, stag scales, #139 .... $295

CENTOFANTE, FRANK Lockback bootknife, 3⅞″ closed, nickel silver bolsters, liners and caps, ivory scales, #12, very fine $385

CENTOFANTE, FRANK Lockback bootknife, 3⅞″ closed, nickel silver bolsters, liners and caps, exhibition grade pearl scales, #16, very fine $435

CENTOFANTE, FRANK Lockback bootknife, 3⅞″ closed, nickel silver bolsters, liners and caps, ivory scales $385

CENTOFANTE, FRANK Lockback bootknife, 4″ closed, nickel silver bolsters, liners and caps, exhibition grade pearl scales $435

CENTOFANTE, FRANK Lockback, 3⅜" closed, nickel silver liners and bolsters, beautiful mother of pearl scales $355

CENTOFANTE, FRANK Lockback, 3½" closed, stainless bolster and liners, black Micarta slabs, satin finish, serial #37 .... $225

CENTOFANTE, FRANK Lockback, 3½" closed, nickel silver liners and bolster caps, #2, cape buffalo horn scales, #2 of this model made long after #1771, matches current quality $335

CENTOFANTE, FRANK Lockback, 3½" closed, nickel silver liners, and bolster caps, exhibition grade pearl scales, serial #038, very fine $425

CENTOFANTE, FRANK Lockback model FL-3, 3½" closed, nickel silver liners and bolsters, ivory scales $375

CENTOFANTE, FRANK Rear lock, 3½" folded, nickel silver bolsters and caps, ironwood scales, very fine little knife $295

CENTOFANTE, FRANK Lockback, 3¾" closed, nickel silver bolsters, perfectly matched stag scales $325

CENTOFANTE, FRANK Lockback, 4" closed, stainless bolsters and liners, red jigged bone scales, satin finish $375

CENTOFANTE, FRANK Lockback, 4⅛" closed, nickel silver bolster, pins and liners, cocobolo scales, satin finish, serial #51 .... $345

CENTOFANTE, FRANK Lockback, 4¼" closed, nickel silver bolsters and liners, ivory scales, serial # 1, Frank's very first lockback makes this a remarkable benchmade knife $435

CENTOFANTE, FRANK Lockback, 4½" closed, stainless bolsters, burgundy Micarta scales, serial #3 .... $140

CENTOFANTE, FRANK Lockback, 4⅝" closed, stainless bolsters, black Micarta handles, serial #3 .... $155

CENTOFANTE, FRANK Slipjoint one-blade, 3¾" closed, ivory Micarta handle, serial #3 ..... $155

CENTOFANTE, FRANK Slipjoint one-blade, 4" closed, brass liners, ivory Micarta handle, serial #3 .... $155

CHALLENGE CUTLERY (ENGLAND) 5¾" blade, nickel silver hilt, stag handle, old and used, no sheath $70

CHALLENGE CUTLERY (ENGLAND) Bowie, 7¼" blade, nickel silver hilt, stag scales, modern sheath, nice old knife $75

CHAMBERG Two-blade Wharncliffe, 4" closed, brass liners, fancy nickel silver bolsters, stag scales, used $30

CHAPPEL, ROD Dagger, 4¾" blade, brass hilt and butt, canvas Micarta handle $515

CHAPPEL, ROD Skinner, 4¼" blade, engraved brass hilt and butt, cocobolo handle $385

CHASE Camp, 3⅞" blade, nickel silver hilt, coral liners, tapered tang, stag slabs, satin finish $175

CHASE Camp, 6" blade, brass hilt, exotic wood handle, no sheath $130

CHEATHAM Dagger, 5⅝" blade, nickel silver and turquoise hilt, butt and sheath trim, iron wood handle, split sheath seam $285

CHEATHAM ST-9 chipped-flint hunter, 4" blade, brass hilt and butt, stag handle, serial #59 .. $195

CINQUIDEA Maker unknown, 12" blade with 6 fullers on each side, hilt 3¼" wide, cast handle and hilt, brass trimmed sheath, very nice work .. $155

CLAY, J.D. ATS 34, 3" blade, nickel silver pins and inlay, ivory Micarta slabs, satin finish, red liners, no sheath $85

CLAY, J.D. Drop point, 2½" tapered-tang mirror polished blade, nickel silver hilt, burgundy liners, yellow Micarta handle, scrimmed rabbit by maker $155

CLAY, J.D. Lockback, 3¼" closed, nickel silver bolsters and liner, mother of pearl scales $235

CLAY, J.D. Trout and bird, 3⅞" blade, nickel silver bolsters, inlay ivory Micarta scales $175

CLAY, WAYNE 3⅞" hollow ground blade, very tapered tang, stainless hilt, pins and thong hole, snakewood scales, red liners, mirror finish, new $175

CLAY, WAYNE 4¼" hollow ground mirror polish blade, very tapered tang, stainless hilt, pins and thong hole, snakewood scales, red liners, new $155

CLAY, WAYNE Drop point hunter, 3½" hollow ground mirror polish blade, very tapered-tang, stainless hilt, pins and thong hole, snakewood scales, red liners $175

CLAY, WAYNE Lightweight lockback, 4¾" closed, aluminum bolsters and liners, black Micarta slabs, mirror finish blade, unused $225

CLAY, WAYNE Lockback, 2¾" closed, stainless bolsters and liners, snakewood scales $195

CLAY, WAYNE Lockback, 3⅞" closed, mirror finish ATS 34 blade, aluminum bolsters and liners, stag slabs $235

CLAY, WAYNE Lockback, 4⅞" closed, engraved aluminum bolsters, red liners, stag scales .. $255

COLEMAN, V.W. Hunter, 3" blade, nickel silver hilt, stag scales $145

COLEMAN, V.W. Hunter, 3⅝" blade, nickel silver hilt, stag scales, nice little knife $165

COLES (NY) Two-blade sleeveboard, 3⅝" closed, brass liners, nickel silver bolsters, pins and thong hole, stag slabs, blade etched Hand Forged $125

COLES (GERMANY) Three-blade premium stock, 4" closed, brass liners, nickel silver bolsters, pins and inlay, stag slabs, blade etched Hand Forged $75

COLES (GERMANY) Three-blade Wharncliffe whittler, 3⅝" closed, nickel silver bolsters, brass liners, fine pearl scales $145

COLES (NY) Three-blade whittler, 4" closed, brass liners, nickel silver bolsters, pins and inlay, stag slabs, blade etched Hand Forged $75

COLES (GERMANY) 3⅝" closed 4 blade congress, nickel silver bolsters and inlay, brass liners, stag scales $80

COLE (GERMANY) Premium stock, 3¼" closed, brass liners, nickel silver bolsters and inlay, stag slabs, blade etched Hand Forged $65

COLLINS Bowie, 12½" blade made from cut-down Collins #858 Machete, brass hilt and butt, stag handle, no sheath, very pitted $50

COLLINS Hand ax, wood handle, red blade $35

COLLINS Homestead axe, 5⅝" blade 11½" wood handle, blue $35

COLLINS AND CO. Axe, 5¼" black blade, 11½" wood handle $40

COLLINS AND CO. Spanish American War Jungle knife, 15" ¼"-stock blade, iron ring rosewood handle, brass trimmed sheath $195

COLLINS, BLACKIE Belt buckle (one of Blackie's handmade originals he sold for $100 at 1970s Kansas City Knife Makers Guild shows, size 38 belt cracked from wrapping around buckle $145

COLLINS, BLACKIE Combat Master, 7½" blade, black zytel hidden compartment hollow handle, camouflage sheath, new $80

COLLINS, BLACKIE Single edge Ninja, 4″ blade, zytel handle $115

COLLUM AND DUFF Drop point, 3¾″ blade, brass trim, ivory Micarta handle $150

COLOBRI Gentleman's stainless one-blade scissors and file, 3″ closed, gold finish engraved handle $30

COLONIAL Two-blade serpentine jack, 3¼″ closed, brass liners and tips, Wrigley's building and Grant Park Chicago plastic handle $35

COLT 6½″ blade, brass hilt, butt and inlay, wood scales, blade engraved Sam Colt The Guns That Won The West, wood presentation box, new $275

COLT Barry Wood swivel-lock, 4⅜″ closed, brass liners, burgundy Micarta scales, leather sheath, box $355

COLT Barry Wood swivel-lock, 4¼″ closed, burgundy linen Micarta scales, used but not worn, belt pouch $185

COLT Barry Wood swivel-lock, 4⅜″ closed, burgundy linen Micarta scales, carried and used but not worn, leather belt pouch, box $245

COLT-BOKER (GERMANY) Lockback, 4¾″ closed, stainless bolsters and liners, blade etched Colt, black (hard rubber?) scales $105

COMBS Boot knife, 4½″ blade nickel silver hilt pins ivory Micarta scales $185

COMBS Prototype sliding dagger belt buckle, 3¾″ blade, knife fight in progress etched in gold inside cover by Shaw-Liebowitz $395

CONNOR Midlock, 3 13/16″ closed, damascus blade, nickel silver bolsters, filework liners and blade, wood scales $150

COOPER 6¼″ ⅜″-thick steel blade, brass hilt and butt, brown Micarta handle, a monster $695

COOPER Cooks, 8⅜″ blade, brass bolster and butt, brown Micarta handle, no sheath $245

COOPER Dagger, 5½″ blade, brass hilt and butt, Micarta handle $355

COOPER Kitchen, 4¾″ blade, brass hilt and butt, brown Micarta handle, no sheath, made by John Cooper for His doctor, used $225

COOPER Kitchen or carver, 10″ blade, brass hilt and butt, brown Micarta handle, no sheath, used, made for John's doctor $320

COOPER Mini bowie, 3⅛″ blade, brass hilt and butt brown, Micarta handle, Eagle Mark made by John Cooper for his doctor, no sheath $295

COOPER Mini bowie, 3½" blade, brass hilt and butt brown Micarta handle, black Micarta spacer $275

COOPER Mini bowie, 3½" blade, brass hilt and butt, brown Micarta handle $295

COOPER Mini bowie, 3½" blade, brass hilt and butt, brown Micarta handle $275

COOPER Skinner, 4¾" blade, brass hilt and butt, black Micarta handle, no sheath, blade varnished but never used $385

CORBY Drop point, 3¼" blade, engraved nickel silver bolsters, ivory scales $195

CORBY Bootknife, 3⅞" blade, engraved nickel silver hilt, ivory Micarta scales $175

CORBY Bootknife, 4¾" blade, engraved brass hilt, ivory Micarta scales $165

CORBY Bootknife, 5" blade, nickel silver hilt and subhilt, ivory Micarta scales $365

CORBY Clip point utility, 4⅜" blade, tapered tang, rosewood scales $95

CORBY Drop point, 3⅞" blade, engraved nickel silver hilt, ivory Micarta scales, big horn ram on one $175

CORBY Drop point, 4½" blade, engraved brass hilt and pins, ivory scales, turquoise inlay both sides $255

CORBY Drop point, 4½" blade, engraved brass hilt and pins, perfectly matched stag scales $225

CORBY Drop point, 4⅝" blade, engraved nickel silver hilt and pins, yellow Micarta handle with maroon lines, no sheath $225

CORBY Drop point, 4¾" blade, engraved brass hilt, ivory Micarta scales, very nice scrimmed leaping swordfish on one $175

CORBY Drop point, 4¾" blade, engraved nickel silver hilt and pins, ivory scales, pair of pheasants scrimmed by wildlife artist Michael Collins on one $345

CORBY Fighter, 5½" blade, engraved nickel silver hilt and sub-hilt, ivory Micarta scales $195

CORBY Fighter, 6½" clip point blade, tapered tang, nickel silver hilt and sub-hilt, yellow Micarta scales, #06 .... $395

CORBY Fighter, 8" blade, nickel silver hilt, subhilt and pins, really great ironwood scales, nicely engraved hilt and subhilt $495

CORBY Fighter, 8" bowie blade, engraved brass hilt, ironwood handle $325

CORBY Loveless-style fighter, 5⅝" blade, nickel silver hilt and subhilt, green Micarta scales $475

CORBY Skeleton bootknife, 4" blade $95

CORDOVA Crooked skinner, 5" blade, brass hilt, black Micarta scales $245

CORDOVA Drop point, 3½" blade, stainless steel hilt, stag scales $175

CORDOVA Drop point, 4" blade, stainless steel hilt, burgundy Micarta scales $145

CORDOVA Fighter, 5½" blade, brass hilt and pins, very fancy figured briar handle, sheath needs snap $245

COURTNEY 3¾" filework blade, brass pins, stag slabs, no sheath, used $50

COURTNEY 3¾" blade, black Micarta slabs $60

COURTNEY 5⅝" Jambiya blade, fileworked tang, wood handle $90

COURTNEY 5¾" blade, wood slab, used $75

COURTNEY Bowie, 7" blade, brass hilt and pins, wood scales $210

COURTNEY Bootknife, 3¼" blade, rosewood scales $60

COURTNEY Bootknife, 4" blade, Micarta scales $60

COURTNEY Bowie, 8" blade, brass hilt and butt, stag handle, no sheath $135

COURTNEY Dagger, 6" blade, brass hilt and butt, exotic handle material $120

COURTNEY Fighter, 6" blade, brass hilt, wood scales $155

COURTNEY Fighter, 7" blade, wood scales, sharpened $165

COURTNEY Fillet, 8¾" satin finish blade, brass pins, new $70

COURTNEY Lebo, 6⅝" satin finish blade, brass hilt, purple stag handle, new $135

COURTNEY Skeleton, 6" blade, wrapped chute cord handle, all black $110

COURTNEY Survival skeleton, 5½" blade, nylon wrap $125

COURTNEY Survival, 6" sawtooth blade, cord wrapped handle, used $85

COURTNEY Upswept skinner, 7" blade, brass pins, wood handle $85

COURTNEY Upswept skinner, 9" blade, wood slabs, brass pins, no sheath $145

COX 3½" fileworked blade and tang, bead blasted, African blackwood ivory Micarta handle, scrimmed duck head, new $195

COX Drop point skinner, 2¾" hollow ground blade, nickel silver hilt, ivory Micarta scales $145

COX Fighter, 7¼" clip point blade, nickel silver hilt and sub hilt, ivory Micarta slabs $275

CRABTREE Drop point skinner, 4" blade, stainless hilt and butt, finger groove stag handle $155

CRAFTSMAN Sears 100th Anniversary large trapper, 4⅜" closed, nickel silver bolsters and inlay, brass liners, jigged bone scales, serial #5210, wooden display box $85

CRAFTSMAN (USA) Sleeveboard lobster pen, 2¾" closed, two blades and manicure tool, very fine pearl scales $115

CRAWFORD 3⅞" hollow ground clip point blade, engraved hilt, oosic scales, filework tapered tang, red liners, mirror finish, new $245

CRAWFORD 4⅝" closed, all steel, bead blasted finish, brass button on blade $115

CRAWFORD Bootknife, 3⅞" blade, nickel silver hilt engraved by Fred Harrington, black Micarta handle, ivory Micarta inlay with scrimmed spider, mirror finish, made 1980 new $225

CRAWFORD Bootknife, 4" blade, brass hilt, walnut handle, serial #14, made 1976 .... $135

CRAWFORD Bootknife, 4¼" bead blasted blade and hilt, filework tang, burgundy liners, black Micarta handle, new $225

CRAWFORD Bootknife, 4½" blade, stainless pins, red liners, very tapered tang, #132, mirror finish, mint $225

CRAWFORD Clip point bootknife, 4¼" blade, file worked tapered tang, nickel silver hilt, stag scales $175

CRAWFORD Fighter, 7" satin finish blade, stainless hilt, red liners, tapered tang, stag slabs, mint $285

CRAWFORD Frame lock (opens and closes one-handed), 4" closed, all stainless steel $125

CRAWFORD Frame lock (opens and closes one-handed), 4⅛" closed, black blade and handle $135

CRAWFORD Lockback, 4⅛" closed, nickel silver liners and bolsters, black Micarta scales $135

CRAWFORD Lockback, 4½" closed, stainless bolsters, red liners, black Micarta handle, new $175

CRAWFORD Mini bootknife, 3″ blade, nickel silver hilt, maple handle, serial #119, made 1976 .. $165

CRAWFORD One-hand knife, 3⅝″ closed, all stainless steel handle, brass button on mirror finish blade, light weight $135

CRAWFORD Pen-style letter opener, 2⅝″ closed, engraved metal case, mirror finish $55

CRIPPLE CREEK One-blade barlow, 3½″ closed, nickel silver bolster and inlay, brass liners, green jigged bone scales, satin finish, blade etched Famous Americans Jim Thorpe All American Athlete, new $50

CRIPPLE CREEK One-blade barlow, 3½″ closed, stainless bolsters, brass liners and pins, bone scales, bolsters stamped Nutmeg State, blade etched Honoring Over 160 years of Connecticut Knifemaking, satin finish $115

CRIPPLE CREEK One-blade swell center, 4½″ closed, nickel silver bolsters, brass liners, brown jigged bone scales, etched $105

CRIPPLE CREEK Two-blade barlow, 3½″ closed, engraved nickel silver bolsters, jigged delrin scales, brass liners, etched Fort City Knife Coll. 1983, #68 of 135 .... $125

CRIPPLE CREEK Two-blade jack, 3⅝″ closed, nickel silver bolsters and inlay, brass liners, jigged bone scales, etched blade, box, new $125

CRIPPLE CREEK Two-blade jack, 3⅝″ closed, nickel silver bolsters and inlay, brass liners, green jigged bone scales, blade etched Green River Rendezvous $125

CRIPPLE CREEK Two-blade Wharncliffe jack, 3⅞″ closed, nickel silver bolsters and inlay, brass liners, jigged bone scales, red etched Half Breed, satin finish $75

CRIPPLE CREEK Wharncliffe whittler, 3¾″ closed, nickel silver bolsters, brass liners, bone scales, engraved Chicago Knife Show, new $90

CRIPPLE CREEK (USA) Two-blade trapper, 3¾″ closed, nickel silver bolsters, inlay, stag scales marked Soy Knife Collectors, 1985, Decatur, IL, 1 of 24, serial #12 .... $195

CRIPPLE CREEK (USA) Three-blade cattleman, 3¾″ closed, nickel silver bolsters and inlay, brass liners, jigged bone scales marked Soy Knife Collectors 1986 Decatur, IL 1 of 23, serial #14 .... $150

CRISNER INDIAN HEAD (SOLINGEN) Premium stock, 3¾" closed, nickel silver bolsters, brass liners, pink, blue, and gold metallic celluloid scales, blade etched Indian Head Handmade Germany $75

CROCKFORD, J. Lockback, 6¾" closed, brass liners, nickel silver bolsters, folding brass guard, locks when open with handle extension that folds into stag handle $200

CROWELL 9¾" bowie blade, brass hilt India stag handle, sharpened but not used $325

CUT-DOWN BAYONET 8" blade, wood handle, steel hilt and butt, no sheath $25

CUTE Chute, 6" blade, brass hilt, black Micarta scales, bead blasted finish $155

D

DAGGET Dagger, 4" blade, nickel silver hilt and sheath, mother of pearl scales, very nice little dagger $375

DAGGET Dagger, 7" blade, nickel silver trim on sheath and knife, African blackwood handle $595

DAGGET Drop point, 3⅛" 440C blade, nickel silver bolsters, sterling silver, desert ironwood scales, badger paw inlay both sides $295

DAGGET Drop point skinner, 3½" blade, tapered tang, nickel silver hilt, rosewood handle, new $155

DAGGET Letter opener or pillow dagger, 8" armor piercing point blade, sterling silver handle with inset amethyst, no sheath, zipper case, fit for a queen $2,445

DAN-D (DENNEHY) Bowie, ⅛" thick satin finish blade, nickel silver hilt, stag scales, new, sheath monogrammed W.E.D. $500

DAN-D (DENNEHY) Fighter, 8" blade, brass hilt and butt, brown Micarta handle $245

DANIELS Bowie, 10" satin finish blade, nickel silver hilt, butt and pins, ivory Micarta scales, new $395

DARBY 3¼" blade, tapered tang, stainless hilt, African Blackwood handles $130

DARBY 3½" Stellite utility blade, black Micarta scales, very thinly ground, a knife for a pro $240

DAVID, G. (FRANCE) Rear lock Laguiole, 4¼" closed, brass bolsters and liners, horn scales $35

DAVIS, C. Hunter, 4½" 440C blade, brass hilt, celluloid handle with pearl inset in butt, brass inlay sheath $115

DAVIS, W.C. Fighter, 4¾" blade, green canvas Micarta handle, very nice knife $185

DAVIS, W.C. 4" bootknife blade nickel silver hilt ivory scales $220

DAVIS, W.C. 4½" clip point ATS34 blade, bead blasted kingwood handles $80

DAVIS, W.C. Lockback, 3⅝" closed, saber ground blade, alloy frame, briar scales $155

DAVIS, W.C. Lockback, 3¾" closed, brass frames, ivory Micarta inserts $155

DAVIS, W.C. Semi-skinner, 3⅞" ATS34 blade, self hilt, brown Micarta scales $85

DAVIS, W.C. Lockback, 4" closed, brass frames, burgundy Micarta scales $95

DAVIS, W.C. Lockback, 4⅛" closed, brass frames, burgundy Micarta scales $95

DAVIS, W.C. Lockback, 4¾" closed, brass frames, black Micarta scales $105

DAVIS BROTHERS 3⅜" 154CM blade, stainless hilt, wood Micarta scales $130

DAWSON Front linerlock, 5" closed, brass button on blade, black Micarta handle black, belt sheath $135

DE LEON 3½" gut hook blade, ivory Micarta scales $140

DE LEON Lockback, 4⅝" closed, brass liners and bolsters, stag scales, leather belt sheath $265

DENT, D.M. 3¼" blade, nickel silver hilt, pins and thong hole, black liners, stag slabs, mirror finish $155

DENT, D.W. Drop point, 4" blade, nickel silver hilt inlay and pins, exotic wood scales $225

DEW, NORMAN Hunter, 6¼" blade, brass hilt and butt, exotic wood handle, used, rare $155

DEW, NORMAN Skinner, 6" blade, brass hilt and butt, wood finger groove handle, unused, rare $295

DIGBY'S KELHAM Slipjoint, 2¾" closed, fancy filework brass liners and back, pearl scales $75

DOWELL, T.M. Dirk, 4½" blade, tapered tang, integral hilt, stag slabs, new $875

DOWELL, T.M. 4¼" blade, stainless frame, ivory Micarta inlay, mirror finish, mint $775

DOWELL, T.M. 5¼" blade, brass hilt, curly myrtle handle, mint $195

DOWELL, T.M. Drop point, 3⅝" blade, very tapered tang, red liners, cocobolo slabs, lightweight $255

DOWELL, T.M. Drop point, 3¾" D-2 blade, nickel silver hilt, burgundy Micarta scales $265

DOWELL, T.M. Drop point, 4" blade, nickel silver hilt and pins, India stag handle $275

DOWELL, T.M. Drop point, 4¼" blade, integral hilt and butt, fancy cocobolo handle sterling and turquoise bear tracks inlays $795

DOWELL, T.M. Funny folder, 4½" closed, D-2 steel blade, stainless screws and inlay, burgundy Micarta slabs, very nice condition $225

DOWELL, T.M. Kitchen or fillet, 8" blade, very tapered tang, red liners backlighting smooth big horn sheep horn handle, nickel sil er pins, very rare $375

DOWELL, T.M. Lightweight drop point hunter, 3½" blade, self hilt, ivory Micarta scales $225

DOWELL, T.M. Pre-Loveless clip point, 5" blade, brass hilt, India stag handle $225

DOWNING, T.W. 4⅝" blade clip point fighter, stainless hilt and pins, stag scales, red liners, tapered tang, hollow ground blade, mirror polish finish, new $295

DOWNING, T.W. Fighter, 4½" blade, stainless hilt and pins, ironwood scales $195

DOWNING, T.W. Fighter, 6⅜" blade, stainless hilt, subhilt and pins, rosewood handles $195

DOWNING, T.W. Hunter, 4⅝" hollow ground blade, tapered tang, stainless hilt, pins and thong hole, ivory scales, red liners, mirror polish finish, new, very nice $395

DOWNING, T.W. Tanto, 4¼" blade, nickel-silver bolster, very nice bird's eye wood scales, both right and left hand sheaths $145

DOWNING, T.W. Tanto, 5½" bead-blasted blade, stainless bolster black Micarta scales $165

DOZIER 5½" 01 steel blade with Borchardt pistol with stock etched by Shaw-Liebowitz, brass hilt and butt etched with initials of Michael Reese (at that time Luger Editor of Guns and Ammo magazine), rosewood handle, no sheath, made about 1968 and etched two or three years later after some blade pitting, pretty good work for a time when no one had ever heard of Bob Loveless (the earliest Dozier I've seen) $325

DOZIER 3⅝" 154CM utility blade, nickel silver hilt, brass pins India stag handle, made about 1974 .... $455

DOZIER Bowie, 6⅝" blade with Monitor and the Marrimac battle etched by Shaw-Liebowitz, sterling silver hilt and butt, scrimmed ivory handle $445

DOZIER Bowie, 9" handrubbed 440C blade, nickel silver hilt African blackwood and ivory handle $675

DOZIER Drop point, 3¾" blade, nickel silver hilt, ebony handles, no sheath, made about 1970 when Dozier was one of a tiny handful of fine makers $325

DOZIER Drop point, 3¼" 154CM blade, brass hilt, African blackwood scales, one of a kind $395

DOZIER Drop point, 3¾" blade, nickel silver hilt, fiberglass Micarta handles (very dangerous material for the knifemaker to work and so not used now that this is known by any maker with good sense), no sheath $435

DOZIER Hunter, 3½" blade, very tapered tang, brass pins, stag slabs, mirror finish, no sheath $375

DOZIER Model 1 Bayou La Fouche 1988 drop point hunter, 3¾" blade, very tapered tang, nickel silver hilt, black Micarta scales, mirror polish finish, no sheath, new $345

DOZIER Skinner, 4¼" blade, nickel silver hilt, India stag handle, made 1972 .... $295

DOZIER Straight hunter, 3½" blade, nickel silver hilt, very well matched stag scales, no sheath, one of only a tiny handful made in 1973 and engraved .. $515

DRAPER Bird and trout, 4" blade, all steel $175

DRAPER Bowie, 9⅛" blade, stainless hilt and butt, black leather handle, mirror finish $595

DRAPER Clip point hunter Javelina model, 5⅞" blade, stainless steel hilt and butt, black Micarta handle, very rare $355

DRAPER Short sword, 16" blade, stainless hilt and butt, ivory Micarta handle, mirror polish finish, new $825

DRAPER Bowie, 12" blade, stainless hilt and butt, Micarta handle, mirror finish, mint $675

DRAPER Thrower, 5½" blade, all steel, rare $155

DUFF Drop point hunter, 4" blade, nickel silver hilt and butt, brass thong hole, ivory Micarta scales with finger grooves, mirror finish, new $165

DUVALL Bootknife, 3¼" blade, nickel silver hilt, wood scales $110

E

EASLER, R.O. Lockback, 3¼″ closed, stainless frames, very fine pearl scales $300

EASLER, R.O. Slipjoint, 2 15/16 closed, stainless bolster, stag scales $175

EDGE BRAND (SOLINGEN) Three-blade stock, 4″ closed, nickel silver bolsters, liners and inlay, pearl scales, serial #1077, blade etched History of Solingen Knife, original box and papers $75

EDGE BRAND (SOLINGEN) Bowie, 8″ blade marked Arkansas Toothpick, brass hilt aluminum butt, wood handle, never used, some pitting on blade $45

EDGE BRAND (SOLINGEN) Model #445 bowie, 6⅛″ blade, marked Original Bowie Knife, brass hilt, stag scales $25

EDGE, MARK Bowie, 10⅛″ blade, brass hilt, aluminum butt, stag handle, #490, used, deep scratches on blade $40

EK Combat, 6½″ blade, brass hilt, parachute cord handle, new $75

EK Combat, 6½″ blade, brass hilt, parachute cord handle, new in box $80

EK Combat, 6½″ blade, brass hilt, parachute cord handle $80

EK Combat, 6½″ dagger blade, brass hilt and pins, black Micarta scales $100

EK Fighter, 6½″ blade, brass hilt, wood Micarta handle, sharpened but not marked $125

EK Fighter, 6½″ blade, brass screws, black Micarta handle, sharpened $125

ENCE, J.F. 3⅝″ blade integral hilt, brass wrapped tang, ivory scales $220

ENCE, J.F. Bootknife, 3¾″ blade, nickel silver hilt, ebony scales with checkered panels $295

ENCE, J.F. Bootknife, 4⅛″ blade, tapered tang, self hilt, desert ironwood scales, no sheath $195

ENCE, J.F. Bootknife, 3⅝″ blade, nickel silver hilt, stag slabs, tapered tang, mirror finish, very nice $395

ENCE, J.F. Bootknife, 3¾″ blade, tapered tang, nickel silver hilt and pins, ebony scales, engraved by S. Lindsey $445

ENCE, J.F. Dagger, 7½" blade, nickel silver hilt and butt, surface ivory slabs, mirror polish finish, hilt and butt engraved and colored by G. Blanchard in roses and greenery, stainless sheath with mirror finish also engraved, beautiful piece! $2,995

ENCE, J.F. Drop point, 3¾" blade, nickel silver hilt, beaded sterling wire wrapped handle securing spectacular abalone shell scales $465

ENDERS, ROBERT Semi-skinner, 4" file-work damascus blade, nickel silver hilt, stag slabs $130

ENGLAND, MIKE Bowie, 9⅛" blade, brass hilt and butt, India stag handle, no sheath $295

ENGLAND, MIKE Drop point prototype, 3½" blade, integral hilt and butt, matched stag scales . . $265

ENGLAND, MIKE Drop point unique style prototype, 3¾" blade, integral hilt and butt, stag handle $485

ENGLAND, MIKE Oklahoma State Patrol TAC fighter, 6" blade, self hilt, black Micarta handle $145

ENGLAND, VIRGIL Drop point, 3¼" blade, integral hilt, matched stag scales, no sheath $310

ENGLISH 4½" shear steel blade, ivory handle, no sheath, forged when William was king of England, old, remarkable condition $60

ENGLISH British Army Fairbairn-Sykes Commando, 6 11/16" blade, steel hilt marked England, lead handle washed with copper and blackened, marked broad arrow and 2, repointed $55

ENGLISH Dagger, 6⅞" etched blade, stainless engraved hilt and butt, ivory handle, no sheath $150

ENGLISH Fruit, 2⅝" closed, sterling blade and engraved bolsters, filework liners, pearl scales $135

ENGLISH Skean dhu, 3½" blade, hallmarked sterling silver trim on knife and sheath $175

ENID Multi-tool, spoon, fork, corkscrew, etc., 4⅜" closed, nickel silver bolsters, green plastic scales, belt sheath, used $40

ERICKSON, CURT Drop point, 3¾" blade, tapered tang, nickel silver hilt, antique stag slabs, mirror finish $345

EXPLORER Custom drop point, Model #21-092, 3⅞" blade, brass bolsters, burgundy canvas Micarta scales $25

EXPLORER Lockback, 3¾" blade, nickel silver bolsters, brass liner, smooth bone scales cracked at pins, scratch on bolster and scale $15

EXPLORER (JAPAN) Lockback, 4" closed, mirror polish blade, nickel silver bolsters, brass liners, wood Micarta slabs, belt sheath $30

EXPLORER (JAPAN) Turkey Hunter lockback, 4" closed, 440C blade and gut hook, brass bolsters, pins and liners, new $30

EXPLORER (SPAIN) Survival, 5½" blade, steel D guard and cast hollow finger-groove handle, more features than any other survival including wire cutter, plastic sheath $35

EYE BRAND (SOLINGEN) Bowie, 7⅛" blade, brass hilt, stag scales $45

F

FAIRBAIRN-SYKES (ENGLAND) Commando dagger, 6¾" blade, steel handle, all black, used, new tip $35

FECAS, STEVE Bootknife, 4" blade, nickel silver bolster, ivory scales, pocket sheath $155

FECAS, STEVE Bootknife, 4" blade, stainless bolster, stag scales $160

FECAS, STEVE Fighter, 6" blade, engraved stainless bolster, ivory scales, very nice $355

FERGUSON, J.E. 3⅝" ATS-34 blade, brass bolsters, exotic wood scales $125

FERGUSON, J.E. 4⅝" ATS-34 clip point blade, brass hilt and butt cap, hardwood handle, beautiful grind, hand-rubbed, outstanding blade work $175

FERGUSON, J.E. 5" flat-ground (saber-grind) hand-rubbed ATS-34 blade, brass hilt, black Micarta scales $175

FERGUSON, J.E. Hunters axe, 9¾" overall length, 3" ATS-34 cutting edge, brass bolster, wood Micarta handle, hip pocket sheath, very nice $175

FERGUSON, J.E. Skinner, 3⅝" ATS34 blade, brass hilt and butt, tigertail maple handle, new maker to me has a beautiful grind and hand-rubbed finish look for great things $165

FIFE CUTLERY (GERMANY) Four-blade congress, 3⅝" closed, nickel silver bolsters and inlay, milled brass liners, stag scales $120

FIFE CUTLERY (GERMANY) Four-blade congress, 3⅝" closed, nickel silver bolsters, brass liners, stag scales, all four blades marked $120

FISCHER, CLYDE Two-blade swell center jack, 4½" closed, nickel silver bolsters and liners, artificial stag scales, belt sheath, used $250

FISCHER, CLYDE Drop point hunter, 3¾" blade, nickel silver hilt, spacers and butt cap, stag handle $165

FISCHER, CLYDE Drop point, 4⅞" blade, nickel silver hilt and butt, finger grooved oosic handle $265

FISCHER, CLYDE Grandaddy barlow, 4½" closed, nickel silver bolsters, bone scales, belt sheath $135

FISCHER, CLYDE YO Special, 5" blade, brass hilt, butt and spacer, finger-groove wood handle, new $265

FISTER, JIM 4" blade, brass pins, wood scales, used $60

FISTER, JIM 6¼" blade, nickel silver hilt and butt, oosic handle, used $150

FISTER, JIM Camp, 9¼x⅜" mirror finish blade, tapered tang, bois d'arc slabs, brass pins, new $155

FISTER, JIM Clip point fighter, 7" blade, brass pins, black Micarta slabs, used $115

FISTER, JIM Hunter, 6" blade, brass pins, wood slabs, used $75

FLOURNOY, JOE Skinner, 3¾" mirror finish blade, nickel silver pins, ivory Micarta slabs, #70, S-78 .... $85

FOX, PAUL 4" closed, one hand opening and closing, satin finish blade, stainless bolsters and liners, wood slabs, #7 .... $775

FOX, PAUL Frontlock, 5" closed, stainless bolsters and liners, stag slabs, #77, sharpened $475

FRANK, HENRY Lockback, 4" closed, brass bolsters and liners, silver inlay, very well matched India stag scales, fine engraving, made in Whitefish Mountain $2,895

FRANK, HENRY Lockback, 4" closed, nickel silver bolsters and liners, silver inlays, very well matched India stag scales, very fine engraving made in Whitefish Mountain $2,995

FRANKLIN, MICHAEL H. 2½" blade, tapered tang, stainless pins, ivory Micarta slabs, #173, no sheath $100

FRANKLIN, MICHAEL H. Bootknife, 3¼" blade, tapered tang, stainless hilt, stag scales, red liners, new $275

FRANKLIN, MICHAEL H. Bootknife, 3⅞" blade, brass hilt and pins, ivory Micarta scales, #138, early work shows why Mike is a top maker today $220

FRANKLIN, MICHAEL H. Coffin handle swivel-lock bootknife prototype, 4⅜" closed, hand-rubbed satin-finish 440C blade, nickel silver bolsters, rosewood scales $395

FRANKLIN, MICHAEL H. Drop point, 3¼" satin finish Stellite blade, titanium bolster, tapered tang, stag slabs, 1-89 #009, very nice $355

FRANKLIN, MICHAEL H. Drop point, 4" Stellite 6K blade, stainless steel hilt, perfectly matched stag scales $355

FRANKLIN, MICHAEL H. Fighter, 5¾" satin-finish double-edge 989C blade, tapered tang, nickel silver hilt, red liners, stag slabs $395

FRANKLIN, MICHAEL H. Linerlock, 3⅜" closed, satin-finish Stellite blade, blue titanium bolster and liners, stag slabs, made 10/88 .... $525

FRANKLIN, MICHAEL H. Linerlock, 3¾" closed, Stellite blade titanium, liners and bolsters, ivory scales $395

FRANKLIN, MICHAEL H. Linerlock, 3¾" closed, stainless blade, titanium bolsters and liners, sheep horn scales $495

FRANKLIN, MICHAEL H. Linerlock, 4⅛" closed, titanium liners and bolsters, horn scales $445

FRANKLIN, MICHAEL H. Linerlock, 4¼" closed, stainless blades, titanium liners and bolsters, oosic scales $445

FRANKLIN, MICHAEL H. Swivel-lock, 4⅜" closed, satin-finish filework-back Stelite 6K blade, stainless bolsters and fancy filework liners, stag scales $525

FRANKLIN, MICHAEL H. Swivel-lock, 3¾" closed, brass liners, colored titanium bolsters, stag scales $365

FRANKLIN, MICHAEL H. Swivel-lock, 4½" closed, hand-rubbed satin-finish 440C blade, nickel silver bolsters, stag scales $330

FRAZIER, RON Bootknife, 3¼" blade, nickel silver bolsters, pins and milled liners, pearl scales, very nice $160

FRAZIER, RON Slipjoint, 3 5/16" closed, stainless bolsters, coral spacers, ivory scales, minor scratches $150

FREILING Hunter, 4⅞" blade, brass hilt, rosewood handle $75

FROST (JAPAN) Bolsterlock, 4⅛" closed, nickel silver bolsters and caps, brass liners, scrimmed scorpion on smooth bone scales $25

FROST (JAPAN) Lockback, 4" closed, nickel silver bolsters and caps, brass liners, scrimmed black widow spider on smooth bone scales $35

FUKUTA, TAK Drop point, 3¾" blade, stainless hilt, stag scales, Loveless student $165

FULLER, JIM 2¾" spear point 440C blade, green linen Micarta scales, no sheath $50

FULLER, JIM Camp, 7¼" blade, brass hilt, exotic wood handle, used $85

FULLER, JIM Frontlock, 3⅞" closed, file work blade back, nickel silver bolsters, spine and liners, cracked mastodon ivory scales $150

FULLER, JIM Frontlock, 4" closed, nickel silver liners and bolsters, stag scales $175

FULLER, JIM Frontlock, 4¾" closed, stainless liners and bolsters, fileworked stag scales $225

FULLER, JIM Midlock, 3⅞" closed, stainless bolster, filework liners and back, big horn sheep scales, scrimmed tiger $220

FULLER, JIM Small game, 2¾" 440C blade, ivory Micarta scales $60

FULLER, W.T. Frontlock One Hander (Mr. Fuller makes knives with only one hand), 5" closed, nickel silver bolsters and liners, stag scales $345

FUNDERBURG Skinner, 4¼" D2 blade, integral hilt and butt, brown Micarta scales $220

G

GALLIGHER Buffalo skinner, 6" blade, brass hilt and butt, fossil walrus and whale ivory and wood handle, Micarta on wood stand, no sheath .. $165

GALLIGHER Hunter, 7" harpoon blade, brass hilt and butt, fossil walrus and whale ivory handles, handsome wood sea-chest, no sheath $325

GARCIA Survival, 6⅞" blade, hollow aluminum butt and hilt, leather handle, sawtooth blade, used $90

GASTON 4¾" satin finish blade, stainless hilt, very tapered tang, perfectly matched stag scales, custom made sheath by D'Holder $275

GASTON 5" blade, very tapered tang, stainless bolsters and pins, filework liners and blade back, stag slabs, hand-rubbed finish, mint $335

GASTON Bootknife, 3¾" hand-rubbed blade, stainless bolsters, perfectly matched stag scales, engraved by Harry Limmings $475

GASTON Bootknife, 4¼" blade, hand-rubbed, stainless steel bolsters, ironwood scales, very nice $395

GASTON Clip point fighter, 4½" satin finish blade, stainless hilt, oosic scales, tapered tang, new $295

GASTON Dagger, 5" price style (single edge) blade, stainless bolsters, mother of pearl handle, engraved, no sheath, zipper case $375

GASTON Fighter, 5¼" blade, stainless bolster, big horn sheep scales $330

GASTON Fighter, 5⅝" blade, nickel silver hilt, black Micarta scales $255

GASTON Fighter, 7" blade, stainless bolsters, perfectly matched stag scales, engraved by Harry Limmings, very nice (matches next two knives perfectly) $525

GASTON Fighter, 5½" hand-rubbed blade, stainless steel bolsters, perfectly matched stag scales, engraved by Harry Limmings $500

GASTON Fighter, 8¼" hand-rubbed hollow ground blade, stainless bolsters, cocobolo scales (this maker has talent) $475

GASTON Gent's Bootknife, 3¼" satin finish blade, very tapered tang, stainless hilt, stag scales, new $225

GASTON Slipjoint, 4⅝" closed, satin finish blade, stainless bolster and liners, nice pearl scales $250

GENOVESE Bootknife, 4¼" clip point, nickel silver hilt, ivory scales $445

GENOVESE Chute, 5⅝" Loveless style blade, nickel silver hilt, drilled black Micarta scales $395

GERBER 4½" blade, stainless steel hilt and butt, ebony handle, has been sharpened $40

GERBER 6¾" blade, all steel, hilt and butt black steel, orange handle, serial #024214, used . . $135

GERBER Two-blade, 4⅛" closed, stainless frame, brass liners, wood inlay, GERBER Two-blade slipjoint, 4" closed, brass liners, wood slabs $45

belt sheath $45

GERBER BMF model, 9" blade with sawtooth, stainless hilt, skullcrusher butt, rubber handle, compass in sheath $150

GERBER Eddie Bauer bolt action, 4¼" closed, black molded plastic handle, unused $50

GERBER Benchmark Rolox Diamondback, 4¼" closed, bead blasted bolster and blade, black Micarta scales, box, new $225

GERBER Benchmark Rolox Diamondback lockback, 4 7/16" closed, stainless bolsters and blade, cocobolo scales, brown leather sheath, original box $275

GERBER Benchmark Rolox Sidewinder, 2⅞" closed, stainless steel bolsters, black Micarta handles, leather pocket sheath, original box $275

GERBER Benchmark Rolox Viper, 3⅞" closed, bead blasted bolster and blade, black Micarta handles, sheath, original box $230

GERBER Benchmark Rolox Viper, 4" closed, bead blasted bolster and blade, black Micarta scales, box, new $245

GERBER Bolt action survival, 5⅛" closed, zytel handle, two-way swivel cordura sheath system, box, new $60

GERBER Bootknife, 3½" blade, Guardian alloy handle, non-slip cover $40

GERBER Bootknife, 5" satin finish blade, cast aluminum hilt and handle $45

GERBER Bootknife, 5" satin finish sawtooth-back blade, black zytel handle and hilt, new $45

GERBER Drop point, 4" blade, stainless hilt and butt, rosewood handle $50

GERBER First lockback model, 5" closed, checkered walnut handle, leather belt pouch, never carried, never used $185

GERBER Folding lockback sportsman, 5" closed, brass liners, hand checkered walnut handle, pouch with steel, box, 1971 brochure, never used, a rare find $175

GERBER Folding Sportsman II, 4¼" lockback, brass frames, Macassar ebony inlays, box, new $40

GERBER Folding Sportsman III lockback, 5¼" closed, brass frames, jasper handle inlays, engraved by R. Valad, walnut presentation box $175

GERBER Folding Sportsman III lockback, 5¼" closed, stainless liners, brass handle, wood inlays, brown leather sheath, box, new $65

GERBER Folding Sportsman III lockback, 5¼" closed, gold whale etched on blade by Shaw-Liebowitz, brass frames, wood inlays, walnut presentation box $175

GERBER Guardian, 3½" dagger blade, aluminum handle $45

GERBER Guardian, 3½" dagger blade, cast aluminum handle, sharpened $40

GERBER Hunter, 4" blade, brass hilt, Macasser ebony handle, box $40

GERBER LMF model, 6" blade, stainless butt and hilt, rubber handle, cordura sheath $95

GERBER Lockback, 4¼" closed, brass interframe, wood inlays, carried $40

GERBER Lockback, bicentennial etched blade, 4¼" closed, engraved brass frames, stag scales .. $85

GERBER Lockback, 5" closed, brass frames, jasper inlays, serial #494, engraved by R. Valade, display box (hinges broken) $160

GERBER Lockback, 4¼" closed, brass bolsters and liners, stag scales, belt sheath, new $125

GERBER Lockback, 5" closed, brass frames, jade inlays, walnut chest $155

GERBER Lockback, 5" closed, brass frame, inlays, engraved by R. Valade, jade scales, walnut box $185

GERBER Lockback, 5¼" closed, brass frames, Jasper inlays, walnut presentation box $175

GERBER Lockback folding hunter, 5" closed, stainless bolsters and liners, wood scales, box, new $75

GERBER Loveless design lockback, 3⅞" closed, black delrin inlay with scrimshaw of eagle in white, nylon pouch, original factory box $125

GERBER Loveless design lockback, 3⅞" closed, nickel-silver frame, rubber inlays, Loveless signature in gold, walnut presentation box, serial #555 of 2,000 .... $225

GERBER Loveless-style, 3⅞" closed, pouch, box, new $115

GERBER Loveless-style lockback, 3⅞" closed, etched blade, steel frame, black checkered inlay, serial #453 of 2,000, wood presentation box $255

GERBER LST Lockback, 3⅝" closed, delrin slabs, handle etched CCI Speer RCBS Outers Omark Ind. $35

GERBER Magnum Folding finger groove lockback Hunter, 4½" closed, brass bolsters and liners, exotic wood scales, belt sheath $75

GERBER Magnum Lockback Folding Hunter, 4½" closed, brass bolsters and liners, rosewood scales, box, new $75

GERBER MK I bootknife, 5" blade, serial #9034 .... $65

GERBER MK I bootknife, 5" dagger blade, aluminum handle, sharpened, never used $45

GERBER MK II first version, 6⅞" dagger blade, alloy handle gray and black trim, original Vietnam era example, never carried, mint $225

GERBER MK II very early, serrations on 6¾" dagger blade, cast aluminum handle in black and gray, serial #023404 .... $195

GERBER MK II second version, serrations on blade, serial #51782, gray and black handle, green sheath $175

GERBER MK II Presentation dagger, 7" blade, brass hilt and butt, Macassar ebony handle, serial #476 .... $175

GERBER MK II Presentation dagger, 7" blade, no serrations, brass hilt and butt, zebra wood handle, serial #477 .... $175

GERBER MK II, 7" dagger blade, aluminum handle with Armorhide coating $45

GERBER MK II, 20th Anniversary 1966-86, 6¾" satin finish blade marked XX1936, gray steel handle, black steel butt and hilt, sheath, box $150

GERBER Model C325 drop point hunter, 3¾" blade, brass hilt, green nylon handle, box, new (discontinued, very hard to find) $30

GERBER Model 400 skinner, 4⅛" blade, stainless hilt and butt, brass spacers, wood scales $75

GERBER PAUL Button lock, 3½" closed, all stainless, first production run, no number inside handle $205

GERBER PAUL Button lock, 3½" closed, stainless steel handles, first production run, no number inside, very rare $225

GERBER PAUL Button lock, 3½" closed, stainless steel liners, cocobolo scales, first production run, no number inside, very rare $235

GERBER PAUL Button lock, 3½" closed, stainless steel liners, ivory Micarta scales, first production run, no number inside handle, very rare $235

GERBER PAUL Button lock, 3½" closed, all stainless steel, first production run, no number stamped inside, plastic presentation box $200

GERBER PAUL Button lock, 3½" closed, satin finish blade etched A & F Co., rosewood scales, no number, box, new $335

GERBER PAUL Button lock, 3½" closed, all stainless steel, no number, box, new $245

GERBER PAUL Button lock, 3½" closed, satin finish blade, cocobolo slabs, leather sheath, first year of production $225

GERBER PAUL Button lock, 3½" closed, all stainless steel, first year, box $205

GERBER PAUL Button lock, 3½" closed, cocobolo handles, first year, box $240

GERBER PAUL Button lock, 3½" closed, ivory Micarta scales, first year, brown leather pouch, bag, ... $255

GERBER PAUL Button lock, 3½" closed, stainless handles, first year, 1 of 100, made for M & M Ferris $225

GERBER PAUL Button lock, 3½" closed, rosewood scales, first year, brown leather pouch, bag $255

GERBER PAUL Button lock, 3½" closed, all stainless, first year of production, box, new $265

GERBER PAUL Button lock, 3½" closed, 40th anniversary of Gerber, first year of Paul (1), serial #1,486, stainless handles $225

GERBER PAUL Button lock, 3½" closed, stainless liners, ivory and Micarta scales, stamped number 2 inside handle, plastic box, mint $175

GERBER PAUL Button lock, 3½" closed, cocobolo overlay, stamped number 2 inside stainless handle, cardboard box, acetate sleeve $225

GERBER PAUL Button lock, 3½" closed, all stainless model, stamped number 2 inside handle ... $175

GERBER PAUL Button lock, 3½" closed, cocobolo overlay, stamped number 3 inside stainless steel handle, cardboard box, acetate sleeve $225

GERBER PAUL Button lock, 3½" closed, ivory Micarta slabs, 4th year of production, in leather pouch sheath, new $230

GERBER PAUL Button lock, 3½" closed, stainless steel, ivory Micarta scales, ducks in field scrimshaw, stamped number 5 inside handle, new $265

GERBER PAUL Button lock, 3½" closed, cocobolo overlay, stamped number 7 inside stainless steel handle, cardboard box, acetate sleeve $195

GERBER PAUL Button lock, 3½" closed, blade etched Final Edition, stainless liners, 8th year (8) inside factory scrimmed black delrin handle, #970 of 1000 .... $175

GERBER PAUL Button lock, 3½" closed, blade etched Final Edition 1986, stamped number 8 inside stainless steel handle, black delrin overlay scrimmed Gerber Factory, cardboard box, acetate cover $235

GERBER PAUL Button lock, 3½" closed, ivory Micarta onlays, brown leather sheath, used $105

GERBER PAUL Button lock, 3½" closed, ivory Micarta scales, box, new $255

GERBER PAUL Button lock, 3½" closed, ivory Micarta scales, brown leather pouch sheath $235

GERBER PAUL Button lock, 3½" closed, stainless steel liners, ivory $175

GERBER PAUL Limited Edition 40th Anniversary Signature Knife, 3½" closed, all stainless steel, etched handle, first year, serial #1,485 of 2,500, box $295

GERBER President's Collection, set of three: 5¼" closed, 4¼" closed and 3½" closed, brass bolsters and liners, stag slabs, presentation box, new $350

GERBER Presentation-grade hunter, 4¾" blade, stainless hilt and butt, walnut handle, box, new $65

GERBER Silver Knight lockback, 3¼" closed, nickel silver bolsters, brass liners, exotic wood scales $30

GERBER Utility, 3⅝" mirror finish blade, ebony handle $65

GILBREATH, RANDALL Fighter, 5⅛" damascus blade, brass bolster and hilt, stag scales, a Parker Edwards knife $155

GILBREATH, RANDALL Linerlock, 3⅞" closed, file-work 440C blade, satin finish, titanium bolsters and liners, ivory slabs, very nice $595

GILBREATH, RANDALL Lockback, 4⅛" closed, nickel-silver bolsters and liners, exotic wood scales $155

GILLENWATER, E.E. (DICK) Lady's Knife, 3¼" mirror finish C-10 blade, very tapered tang, stainless hilt and pins, rosewood Micarta scales, new $165

GILLENWATER, E.E. (DICK) Low Country Filet, 6" blade, very tapered tang, mirror finish, stainless hilt and pins, rosewood Micarta scales, serial #003, Best of Show - 1983 Guild makers NY $125

GLOVER, RONALD GENE 3½" clip point blade, stainless hilt, Micarta handle $135

GLOVER, RONALD GENE Semi-skinner, 2⅝″ blade, stainless hilt, pins and thong hole, cocobolo scales, new $125

GLOVER, RONALD GENE Semi-skinner, 3½″ satin finish blade, very tapered tang, stainless hilt, ironwood scales, new $195

GODDARD, WAYNE 3⅞″ blade, cable wire damascus handle and blade $175

GODDARD, WAYNE Bowie, 8¼″ blade, brass hilt, butt and pins, walnut scales, new $295

GODDARD, WAYNE Bowie, 9¼″ blade marked Test blade, not for sale, made for Journeyman stamp in ABS, stainless pins, hardwood handle, hand-rubbed finish $280

GODDARD, WAYNE Hunter axe prototype, osage orange handle $295

GODDARD, WAYNE Odin's Claw lockback, 5½″ closed, stainless bolsters and liners, black Micarta scales, belt sheath, new $225

GODDARD, WAYNE Slipjoint, 3″ closed, engraved nickel-silver bolsters and liners, abalone scales, very fine $200

GODDARD, WAYNE Slipjoint, 4⅝″ closed, nickel-silver bolsters and liners, stag scales $200

GODDARD, WAYNE Slipjoint, 5⅝″ closed, nickel-silver liners, bolsters and caps, engraved polished bone scales with turquoise inlays by George Sherwood $275

GOLDING Diver's (first edition), 7⅜″ ATS-34 steel sawtooth blade, black Micarta scales, Kydex sheath, new $125

GOLDING Model 24-S, 4¾″ blade, rosewood scales $125

GOLTZ, WARREN L. Hunter, 3½″ ATS34 steel sawback blade, green canvas Micarta scales, fine, shows real talent $175

GOLTZ, WARREN L. Hunter, 4″ satin finish blade, tapered tang, stainless pins, black Micarta slabs, outstanding $225

GOLTZ, WARREN L. Model 3 drop point hunter, 4⅛″ ATS34 steel blade, black Micarta scales, very high quality work $175

GORDON Bootknife, 4⅛″ blade, cocobolo scales, no sheath $205

GORDON Drop point, 3½″ blade, stainless steel hilt, stag scales, no sheath $135

GORDON Guthook, 3⅝″ blade, stainless steel hilt, burgundy Micarta scales $140

GORDON Model 8 utility hunter, 3¾″ mirror finish blade, tapered tang, stainless hilt and pins, cocobolo scales, serial #485, new $155

GORDON Skinner, 3″ blade, nickel silver hilt, black striped bone Micarta scales $115

GORSKI (GERMANY) 3⅜″ blade, tapered tang, integral bolster, ironwood scales D.F. Kressler style, very fine work $425

GOTTAGE, DANTE & JUDY Western tanto, 8″ parkerized blade, parkerized steel hilt, camo wood/Micarta handle, camo leather sheath $180

GREG Lockback, 3¾″ closed, aluminum frame, ivory Micarta slabs, serial #004, leather belt sheath $75

GRIGG Grandaddy Barlow, 5¼″ closed, nickel silver bolsters, Ivory scales $265

GROHMANN Upswept skinner, 4″ blade, satin finish, brass pins, wood scales, new $35

GROHMANN D.H. Russell, 4″ satin finish blade, wood scales, new $30

GOMPH, H.G. 5¾″ blade, brass hilt, wood handle, no sheath $20

H

HACKMAN (FINLAND) 7″ blade, sawtooth back, nickel-silver hilt and butt cap, hollow handle, stacked-leather-washer grip, custom sheath $145

HAERING (GERMANY) Nazi SA dagger, 8¾″ blade, nickel-silver hilt, butt and sheath trim, wood handle (one side missing small chip) $165

HAGEN, DOC 12½″ forged 10/50 steel blade, copper tsuba, brass pins, fir handle and sheath covered with snakeskin and wrapped with silk cord $395

HAGEN, DOC Drop point skinner, 3¼″ blade, stainless hilt and butt, stag handle, excess glue on hilt and butt $255

HALE, LLOYD 3⅞″ clip point blade, fileworked nickel-silver fittings, all stag handle, stag sheath $565

HALE, LLOYD 4″ clip point, brass hilt, big horn sheep handle (early work by one of today's master makers) $175

HALE, LLOYD 5½" guthook blade, brass hilt and butt, India stag handle $295

HALE, LLOYD (Unmarked) Arkansas Toothpick, 11¾" dagger blade, nickel-silver hilt and butt, abalone in butt, stag ivory cut into a spiral, no sheath. (an outstanding knife) $995

HALE, LLOYD Bootknife, 4½" blade, nickel-silver hilt, yellow Micarta scales, early work by well-known maker $245

HALE, LLOYD Bootknife, 5⅛" blade, brass hilt, black Micarta scales (early work by great maker) $195

HALE, LLOYD Bowie, 9½", brass hilt, ebony scales, crack at one pin, no sheath, new $295

HALE, LLOYD Dagger, 5⅜" hand-lrubbed blade, ivory Micarta scales (small crack one side), very rare signature mark $365

HALE, LLOYD Drop point, 3⅜" blade, brass bolster and butt, India stag handle, no sheath, early work $190

HALE, LLOYD Hunter, 5" 440C guthook blade, nickel-silver hilt and butt, India stag handle, no sheath $275

HALE, LLOYD Midlock, 4⅜" closed, mirror finish 440C blade with brass inlay, nickel-silver bolsters, filework liners, matched stag scales, leather belt sheath $350

HALE, LLOYD Skinner, 5½" filework blade, brass and red hilt spacer, nickel-silver butt cap and hilt, stag handle $265

HALE, LLOYD Skinner, 5⅝" filework blade, nickel-silver hilt and butt cap, stag handle $355

HAMMOND 3¼" skinner blade, nickel-silver bolsters, exotic wood scales $215

HANSON Frontlock, 4⅛" closed, nickel-silver frames, green semi-precious stone inlays, shopworn $315

HARDCASTLE Bird, 2½" blade, brass hilt, ebony handle $120

HARLEY 6¼" blade, self hilt, black Micarta handle, all sandblasted $55

HARLEY (BRISTOL, TN) 7" black blade, tapered tang, camouflage Micarta slabs, new $135

HARRIS Lockback, 3⅞" closed, damascus blade, stainless steel interframe, green inlays, serial #004 .... $395

HARTSFIELD Bowie, 7" blade, steel hilt, wood handle $475

HARTSFIELD Dagger, 6" blade, cocobolo scales $395

HARTSFIELD Fighter, 4⅝" double-edge satin-finish sawtooth blade, black cord handle $295

HARTSFIELD Hunter, 4" blade, rosewood handle $195

HARTSFIELD Strong Boy, 4⅛" etched tanto blade, rope handle, new $495

HARTSFIELD Tanto, 5¼" blade $335

HARTSFIELD Tanto, 12" blade, matched oak handle and sheath $395

HASTINGS Skinner, 4½" blade, forged brass hilt and butt, mesquite handle, mirror finish $295

HEATH Hunter, 5¾" blade, brass hilt and butt, red and white spacers, stag handle $195

HEHN (GERMANY) Interframe slipjoint, 2⅜" closed, stainless damascus blade, stainless frame, exotic wood inlays, fine little knife $295

HELLE (NORWAY) 2¾" satin finish stainless blade, wood handle, brass pins $35

HELLE (NORWAY) 4¼" laminated steel blade, stainless hilt and butt screw, reindeer or moose butt and spacer, birch handle, silver sheath trim $95

HELLER Mini-skinner, 2½" blade, nickel-silver bolsters, burgundy Micarta scales, pocket sheath, nice knife, used $55

HEN & ROOSTER 3⅝" closed, spearpoint blade, coffin handle, nickel-silver bolsters and liners, stag scales $285

HEN & ROOSTER One-blade pen, 3" closed, nickel-silver liners, cattle horn scales $75

HEN & ROOSTER One-blade coffin-handle slipjoint, model 772H, 3⅝" closed, nickel-silver bolsters and liners, cattle horn scales, new $240

HEN & ROOSTER One-blade coffin-handle slipjoint, model 772H, 3⅝" closed, nickel-silver bolsters and liners, cattle horn scales, new $240

HEN & ROOSTER One-blade coffin-handle slipjoint, 3⅝" closed, nickel-silver bolsters and liners, burgundy Micarta scales $215

HEN & ROOSTER One-blade coffin handle slip joint, 3⅝" closed, engraved bolsters, ivory Rucarta $365

HEN & ROOSTER Two-blade congress, 3⅛" closed, nickel-silver bolsters and liners, ivory Micarta scales $125

HEN & ROOSTER Two-blade congress, 3⅜" closed, nickel-silver bolsters brass liners, stag scales $125

HEN & ROOSTER Two-blade congress, model 273H, 3½" closed, nickel-silver bolsters and liners, African cattle horn scales, box $90

HEN & ROOSTER Two-blade even-end lobster and manicure tool, 2⅞" closed, nickel-silver liners, celluloid cattlehorn scales, mint $85

HEN & ROOSTER Two-blade sleeveboard lobster and manicure tool, 2½" closed, nickel-silver liners, African cattle horn scales, mint $160

HEN & ROOSTER Two-blade pen, 2¼" closed, nickel-silver liners, pearl scales, mint, (hard to find) $135

HEN & ROOSTER Two-blade pen, 3¼" closed, nickel-silver liners, cattle horn scales $125

HEN & ROOSTER Two-blade pen, 3¼" closed, engraved stainless handles, nice $105

HEN & ROOSTER Two-blade equal-end pen, 3¼" closed, all stainless steel $105

HEN & ROOSTER Two-blade stock, 4" closed, clip and spay blades, nickel-silver liners and bolsters, coral Rucarta scales $115

HEN & ROOSTER Three-blade Wharncliffe whittler, 1750-E series 111, 3" closed, nickel-silver bolsters, brass liners, ivory scales, minor pitting on back spring $245

HEN & ROOSTER Four-blade congress, 3⅛" closed, brass liners, nickel-silver bolsters, stag scales $230

HEN & ROOSTER Four-blade congress, 3¾" closed, brass liners and nickel-sliver bolsters, stag scales $265

HEN & ROOSTER Multi-blade sportsman, 3½" closed, all stainless steel $265

HEN & ROOSTER Model 111 two-blade even-end jack, 3½" closed, nickel-silver bolsters, pins and liners, stag scales, from the 111 set, very rare, mint $230

HEN & ROOSTER Model 256, A.G. Russell two-blade senator, 3½" closed, nickel-silver bolsters and liners, ivory scales $255

HEN & ROOSTER Model 273 two-blade congress, 2⅞" closed, nickel-silver liners, bolsters, cattle horn $155

HEN & ROOSTER Model CM-6EE, Coffin-handle, 2⅞" saber-ground blade etched with arrow, engraved nickel-silver bolsters, liners and arrow-head inlay, serial #39, Excelsior (non-standard value reference) grade $195

HEN & ROOSTER CM-7 .45 Long Colt vest pocket skinner, 3½" closed, nickel-silver bolsters, liners and cartridge inlay, jacaranda scales, mint $125

HEN & ROOSTER Model CM-7EE, Vest Pocket Skinner, 3½" closed, gold etched blade, engraved nickel-silver bolsters and liners, jacaranda scales, serial #39, Excelsior (non-standard value reference) grade $245

HEN & ROOSTER CM-8 barlow, 2⅞" closed, nickel-silver liners bolsters and cartridge, inlay Grindilla scales $155

HEN & ROOSTER CM-8EE Little Brother Barlow, 2⅞" closed, etched blade, engraved nickel-silver bolster, liner and inlay, African blackwood scales, serial #39 .... $175

HEN & ROOSTER CM-9 .300 savage canoe, 3¼" closed, stainless handles, nickel-silver cartridge inlay, mint $65

HEN & ROOSTER CM-9EE canoe, 3¼" closed, etched blade, engraved stainless scales, nickel-silver cartridge inlay, serial #39 .... $130

HEN & ROOSTER Swell-center pen, 2¾" closed, mother of pearl scales, made in the 1920s, red leather Morocco case $135

HEN & ROOSTER Senator, two blades and cork-screw, 3½" closed, shadow pattern stag scales, pre-WW I European pocket knife, used, shows age $35

HEN & ROOSTER 111th Anniversary Set, 10 knives, old fashioned high carbon steel blades, nickel-silver liners and bolsters, scales of ivory, mother of pearl, stag, and horn. (The ivory and pearl stock knives are worth $800 by themselves) $1,675

HEN & ROOSTER Vest pocket skinner, model 101BR, 3½" closed, nickel-silver bolsters, liners $125

HEN & ROOSTER Vest pocket skinner, model 101CR, 3½" closed, nickel-silver bolsters, liners, coral Rucarta scales, mint $125

HEN & ROOSTER Vest pocket skinner, Model 101IR, 3½" closed, nickel-silver liners, bolsters ivory Rucarta $125

HEN & ROOSTER Vest pocket slipjoint skinner, 3⅜" closed, hollow ground very thin blade, nickel-silver liners and bolsters, India stag scales $175

HEN & ROOSTER Bertram two-blade congress, 3¾" closed, brass liners, nickel-silver bolsters, jigged bone scales, refinished $140

HEN & ROOSTER Bertram two-blade senator, 3¾" closed, brass liners, nickel-silver bolsters, pearl scales $160

HEN & ROOSTER Bertram two-blade serpentine airweight (no liners), 4" closed, coral Rucarta scales, very fine, very rare $175

HEN & ROOSTER Bertram four-blade congress, 3⅜" closed, nickel-silver bolsters, brass liners, pearl scales, used $100

HEN & ROOSTER Bertram four-blade congress, 3¾" closed, brass liners, nickel-silver bolsters, stag scales $195

HEN & ROOSTER Bertram even-end pen, 2⅞" closed, engraved stainless scales $75

HEN & ROOSTER Bertram even-end pocket, 4" closed, engraved stainless scales $85

HEN & ROOSTER Bertram Model AGR KCC CM-6 Straight Arrow coffin, 2⅞ closed, nickel-silver bolsters and liners, flint arrow inlay, stag scales $155

HEN & ROOSTER Bertram Model 607 four-blade lobster senator, 3⅛" closed, shadow pattern with scissors, toothpick and tweezers, pearl scales $295

HEN & ROOSTER Bertram (111th Anniversary) two-blade senator, 2⅞" closed, nickel-silver bolsters and liners, horn scales, serial #234, ... $155

HEN & ROOSTER Bertram (111th Anniversary) sleeveboard whittler, 3½" closed, nickel-silver bolsters, ivory scales, serial #234 .... $385

HEN & ROOSTER Bertram stock, 4" closed, nickel-silver bolsters and inlay, brass liners, stag scales $220

HEN & ROOSTER C. Bertram four-blade congress, 3¾" closed, brass liners, nickel-silver bolsters, black bone scales, pre-World War II, very rare $275

HEN & ROOSTER Carter pen, 3" closed, nickel silver-liners, cracked ice celluloid scales, mint, rare mark $95

HEN & ROOSTER Carter even-end pen, 2⅞" closed, engraved stainless scales $65

HEN & ROOSTER Fife Cutlery Co. four-blade congress, 3¾" closed, brass liners, nickel-silver bolsters and pins, bone scales, used $115

HEN & ROOSTER Gutmann two-blade congress, 3⅜" closed, nickel-silver bolsters, brass liners, stag scales, slightly used $100

HEN & ROOSTER G tmann two-blade stock, 4" closed, nickel-silver bolsters, brass liners, stag scales $225

HEN & ROOSTER Gutmann three-blade stock, 4" closed, nickel-silver bolsters, brass liners, stag scales, never carried, shows some age $195

HEN & ROOSTER Gutmann three-blade stock, 4" closed, nickel-silver bolsters, brass liners, stag scales $355

HEN & ROOSTER Gutmann three-blade Wharncliffe whittler, 3" closed, nickel-silver bolsters, brass liners, stag scales $165

HEN & ROOSTER Gutmann three-blade whittler, 3" closed, nickel-silver bolsters, brass liners, pearl scales, mint, very hard to find $185

HEN & ROOSTER Gutmann four-blade congress, 3⅛" closed, brass liners, nickel-silver bolsters, stag scales, used and repolished $140

HEN & ROOSTER Gutmann four-blade congress, 3⅜" closed, nickel-silver bolsters brass liners stag scales $195

HEN & ROOSTER Gutmann four-blade congress, 3¾" closed, nickel- silver bolsters, brass liners, stag scales $245

HEN & ROOSTER Gutmann four-blade congress, 3¾" closed, nickel- silver bolsters, brass liners, stag scales, used, good $115

HEN & ROOSTER Gutmann premium stock, 4" closed, nickel-silver bolsters, brass liners, stag scales, hard to find $225

HEN & ROOSTER Voss Cutlery Co. two-blade senator, 3¼" closed, nickel-silver bolsters, brass liners, fine pearl scales $145

HEN & ROOSTER Voss Cutlery Co. four-blade congress, 3⅜" closed, nickel-silver bolsters, brass liners, pearl scales $175

HEN & ROOSTER Voss Cutlery Co. four-blade congress, 3⅜" closed, nickel silver bolsters, brass liners, pearl scales, fine condition for a 30 to 60 years old $115

HEN & ROOSTER Voss Cutlery Co. four-blade congress, 3¾" closed, brass bolsters and liners, pearl scales, rust $135

HEN & ROOSTER Voss Cutlery Co. four-blade congress, 3¾" closed, nickel-silver bolsters, brass liners, pearl scales, fine condition for a 30-60 year-old $115

HEN & ROOSTER Voss Cutlery Co. Wharncliffe whittler, 3½" closed, nickel-silver bolsters, stag scales $375

HENCKELS, PAUL A. (GERMANY) 4" closed, satin finish blade, nickel-silver rat tail bolsters and inlay, brass liners, stag scales $125

HENCKELS, PAUL A. (GERMANY) 5¼" satin finish blade, integral hilt and butt, stag inlays with finger grooves, new $125

HENCKELS, PAUL A. (GERMANY) One-blade jack, 3⅜" closed, nickel-silver bolsters, inlay and pins, brass liners, jigged bone scales $45

HENCKELS, PAUL A. (GERMANY) One-blade saber-ground jack, 3⅜" closed, nickel-silver bolsters, inlay and pins, brass liners, stag slabs $45

HENCKELS, PAUL A. (GERMANY) Two-blade pen, 3" closed, nickel-silver bolsters, inlay, stag scales $60

HENCKELS, PAUL A. (GERMANY) Two-blade senator, 3" closed, mirror finish blades, nickel-silver bolsters, inlay, liners, and pins, ivory slabs ... $60

HENCKELS, PAUL A. (GERMANY) Two-blade even-end senator, 3" closed, nickel-silver liners, pins, bolsters and inlay, ivory scales $60

HENCKELS, PAUL A. (GERMANY) Two-blade senator, 4" closed, brass liners, nickel-silver bolsters, yellow celluloid scales, advertising knife, used $85

HENCKELS, PAUL A. (GERMANY) Two-blade trapper, 4" closed, nickel-silver bolsters and inlay, brass liners, jigged bone scales, etched blade, chip from bone $30

HENCKELS, PAUL A. (GERMANY) Three-blade serpentine stock, 3¼" closed, nickel-silver bolsters and shield, black Micarta scales $45

HENCKELS, PAUL A. (GERMANY) Lockback, 4½" closed, nickel-silver bolsters, brass liners, stag scales, shows some shopware $155

HENCKELS, PAUL A. (GERMANY) Lockback with gutting blade, 4¾" closed, nickel-silver bolsters, brass liners, stag scales $125

HENCKELS, PAUL A. (GERMANY) Premium stock, 3⅝" closed, nickel-silver bolsters, stag scales, used $145

HENCKELS, PAUL A. (GERMANY) Pruner, 3⅞" closed, nickel-silver bolster and inlay, brass liners, stag scales $120

HENCKELS, PAUL A. (GERMANY) Stock, 3½" closed, nickel-silver bolsters, liners and inlay, stag scales $125

HENCKELS, PAUL A. (GERMANY) Stock, 3¼" closed, nickel-silver bolsters, liners, and inlay, stag scale $110

HENCKELS, PAUL A. (GERMANY) Stock, 2¾" closed, nickel-silver bolsters, liners, inlay, black scales $60

HENCKELS, PAUL A. (GERMANY) Trick knife, 2⅞" closed, all stainless, handle engraved H. Frei, carried $30

HENCKELS, PAUL A. (GERMANY) Wharncliffe jack, 3⅝" closed, nickel-silver bolsters and inlay, brass liners, yellow celluloid scales $40

HENDRICKS, LARRY 4" hollow ground drop point blade, solid sterling bolsters sculpted with four animals, ivory scales carved in high relief with oak leaves and acorns, wood presentation box $1895

HENDRICKS, LARRY Kangaroo with caper in handle, 3⅝" drop point hollow-ground 154CM blade, stainless hilt, very fine ironwood scales, serial #1 .... $695

HENDRICKS, LARRY Kangaroo with caper in handle, 4¼" drop point blade, stainless steel hilt and butt, ivory Micarta scales $385

HENDRICKS, LARRY Model K2, 4" flat ground hand-rubbed blade, all stainless, serial #142 $550

HENDRICKSON Bowie, 6⅝" forged blade, nickel-silver hilt and butt, sterling wire inlaid in maple handle $215

HENDRICKSON Skinner, 6" blade, nickel-silver hilt, sterling wire inlaid in maple handle $205

HENRY, D.E. Bowie, 7" blade, nickel-silver hilt and wrap, rosewood handle, nickel-silver trimmed sheath $2395

HENRY, D.E. Patch (properly ground flat one side for right handed shooter), 3½" blade, nickel-silver bolster, thong keeper and bullet starter, ebony handle, this has to be the top in patch knives $695

HENSLEY Miniature, 3½" blade, stainless hilt, ivory slab handle with finger grooves, ivory cracked at thong hole $90

HERITAGE SCHRADE 1983 Two-blade jack, 3⅛" closed, nickel-silver bolsters and inlay, brass liners, green jigged bone scales, etched Everlastingly Sharp $35

HERRON Bootknife, 4⅛" blade, stainless steel hilt, black Micarta handles very nice $475

HERRON Bootknife, 4¼" double-ground mirror finish blade, very tapered tang, stainless steel hilt $355

HERRON Bootknife, 4¼" blade, brass hilt and pins, fiddle-back maple handle, made before he began to serial number all his knives, no sheath $275

HERRON Bootknife, 4¼" blade, stainless hilt, ivory scales, etched by famous English engraver Ken Hunt $845

HERRON Drop point, 3½" bead-blasted blade, nickel-silver hilt, well matched India stag scales, never used but shows lots of handling $175

HERRON Drop point, 4½" blade, fox in gold and copper etched by Shaw-Liebowitz,stainless hilt, ivory Micarta scales, #1 .... $395

HERRON Drop point hunter, 4½" 154CM blade, stainless hilt, black Micarta scales $295

HERRON Fighter, 4¼" clip point blade, stainless hilt and pins, black liners, maple scales, new ... $295

HERRON Filet, 6" blade, stainless steel hilt, black Micarta scales, no sheath $175

HERRON Filet/Utility Cheapo, 5" satin finish blade, cocobolo scales, new $75

HERRON Lockback, 4¼" closed, stainless bolsters, stag scales $655

HERRON Lockback, 4⅜" closed, stainless steel bolsters, pink ivory scales, very hard to come by $595

HERRON Lockback, 4 7/16" closed, stainless bolsters, cocobolo scales $595

HERTER Bull Cook's, 4" blade, rosewood handle—Herter's speciality was cheap, sometimes they had something really good, this is one of those things that cost about $1.50 new, now worth $20, the only one I have seen in 20 years $20

HETHCOAT (CLOVIS, NM) Skinner, 3½" hollow ground blade, tapered tang, brass hilt, pins and thong hole, red liners, stag slabs with finger grooves, 87 #195 .... $125

HIBBARD, SPENCER & BARTLETT 4¼" two-blade slipjoint, iron bolsters, brass liners, celluloid scales, good condition but very worn, (for the OVB collector) $70

HIBBEN 3¼" guthook blade, engraved stainless steel hilt and butt, fossilized oosic scales, Alaska mark $285

HIBBEN 4¼" blade, brass hilt, white tail antler handle, early BenHIBBEN mark, pretty crude work from the 60s $155

HIBBEN Bootknife, 4⅜" blade, brass hilt and butt, ivory Micarta handle, Alaska mark, no sheath $180

HIBBEN Bowie, 12½" blade (⅜" stock), stainless hilt, ivory Micarta scales, really massive, huge, no sheath $455

HIBBEN Drop point, 3½" blade, stainless steel hilt, fossilized walrus ivory handle with gold nugget on one side, Alaska mark $345

HIBBEN Drop point, 4" blade, nickel-silver hilt, ivory Micarta scales, Alaska mark $185

HIBBEN Drop point, 4" thumb-rest blade, nickel-silver hilt, oosic scales $295

HIBBEN 8" Parker Fighter (named for Gil's martial arts instructor, a big deal in the early 70s), stainless hilt and butt, stag handle, Star of David engraving $495

HIBBEN Skinner, 4¼" blade, brass hilt and butt, stag handle, made 1982 .... $145

HIBBEN Skinner, 5" blade (¼" stock), stainless hilt and butt, cracked mastodon ivory handle, Alaska mark $295

HIBBEN Thrower, 10" overall, ¼" stock, all steel, no sheath $55

HIBBEN (MANTI) 3½" blade, 7⅛" overall, all steel, no sheath $65

HIBBEN (MANTI) 5⅛" blade, brass hilt and butt, black spacers, hardwood handle, filework blade back, mirror finish, hilt monogrammed RJP $165

HIBBEN (MANTI) 5⅛" clip point blade, brass hilt and butt, walnut handle, hilt monogrammed S.H.S. $175

HILL, RICK Bootknife, 4½" ATS 34 blade, file-worked tang, nickel-silver bolsters, exotic wood scales $175

HILL, RICK Fighter, 7¾" clip point blade, stainless hilt and sub-hilt, red liners, stag slabs, mirror finish, serial #266 .... $315

HILL Fighter (Persuader), 4¼″ blade, steel hilt and butt cap, red spacers, stag handle with finger grooves $155

HOCKEY (GERMANY) Even-end lobster advertising (scissors, nail file, screwdriver and blade) knife, 2¾″ closed, cracked ice celluloid scales with inlay $30

HODGSON, R.J. 4″ upswept skinner blade, brass hilt, rosewood handle with finger grooves, used, no sheath $75

HOEL Interframe lockback, 4″ closed, nickel-silver frames, ivory inlays, serial #243 .... $675

HOEL Interframe lockback, 4″ closed, bronze interframe rosewood inlays $495

HOEL Interframe lockback, 4½″ closed, stainless steel frames, cape buffalo inlays, serial #2 .. $575

HOEL Lockback, 3¼″ closed, nickel-silver liners, green jigged bone shadow pattern covers, a fantastic, very slim little knife $395

HOEL Lockback, 4″ closed, filework spine, nickel-silver bolsters and liners, stag scales, fine early work $495

HOEL Slipjoint, 2¾″ closed, stainless steel liners, bolsters, goldlip pearl scales, filework spring, carried but not sharpened, serial #242 .... $295

HOEL Slipjoint, 3⅛″ closed, stainless steel bolsters, caps and liners ivory scales cracked at one pin, serial #249 .... $395

HOFFMAN Lockback, 4″ closed, nickel-silver bolsters, brass liners, black Micarta scales, serial #46 .... $155

HOFFMAN, D.B. Frontlock, 4¼″ closed, stainless frames, burgundy Micarta scales, serial #2, very nice indeed $245

HOFFMAN, D.B. Lockback, hand-rubbed finished blade, 3¾″ closed, nickel-silver bolsters, burgundy Micarta scales, serial #13 .... $215

HOFFMAN, K.L. Tanto, 6⅛″ bead blasted blade with polished temper line, black Micarta scales, really first class extra custom sheath $175

HOFFRITZ Kissin' Krane premium stock, 3⅞″ closed, nickel-silver bolsters and liners, fine pearl scales $115

HOFFRITZ Kissin' Krane premium stock, 4″ closed, nickel-silver bolsters, brass liners, exhibition grade pearl scales $90

HOLDER, D' 3½″ blade, nickel-silver hilt and butt, ivory and amber handle, small cracks in ivory $245

HOLDER, D' 3¾″ blade, integral bolster, stainless butt, amber handle, beautiful $365

HOLDER, D' Bird and trout, 4″ blade, nickel-silver bolsters, brown Micarta handle with black stripe, very slim $175

HOLDER, D' Caper, 2¼″ blade, stainless hilt, oosic scales, very nice $225

HOLDER, D' Caper, 3″ blade, nickel-silver hilt and butt, amber and pinchoti handle, very nice knife $335

HOLDER, D' Fighter, 6″ blade, nickel-silver hilt and butt, stag handle, very nice $255

HOLDER, D' Fighter, 6¼″ blade, fancy file work all around tang and blade back, very fancy nickel-silver, fancy figure crotch walnut handle ... $535

HOLDER, D' Hunter, 5¾″ 440C blade, nickel-silver hilt and butt cap, ebony handle, no sheath, zippered case, outstanding large hunter by this very talented maker $275

HOLDER, D' Hunter's ax, nickel-silver bolster and butt cap, brown Micarta handle, very nice .. $285

HOLDER, D' Hunter set, 2⅝″ and 2¼″ 440C blades, beautifully matched elk horn scales, double sheath $195

HOLDER, D' Lockback, 3¾″ blade, nickel-silver bolsters and liners, exotic wood scales, fileworked blade back and locking bar, nicest D'Holder folder I have seen $175

HOLDER, D' Lockback, 4¾″ closed, nickel-silver liners, bolsters and caps, fileworked ivory scales inlaid with nuggets of turquoise $200

HOLDER, D' Slipjoint, 3½″ closed, brass bolsters, pins and liners, cocobolo scales $145

HOLDER, D' Slim hunter, 3⅝″ 154CM blade, bronze bolsters engraved by Mel Wood, three-piece amber scales with red spacers, gorgeous $455

HOLDER, D' Semi-skinner, 3½″ 440C blade, nickel-silver hilt, very unusual stag scales $175

HOLSTORM Chute, 4½″ blade, stainless hilt and pins, African blackwood handles $195

HORN 3″ 154CM blade, nickel-silver bolsters and caps, engraved by Juli Warenski and inlaid with gold, perfect ivory scales, #3 .... $1,285

HORN Two-blade pen, 3¼″ closed, nickel-silver bolsters and liners, very fine mother of pearl scales, #18 .... $1595

HORN Two-blade pocket, 3⅛″ closed, nickel-silver bolsters and liners, perfect ivory scales, #25 $755

HORN American Bicentennial 1776-1976 lockback, 3¾" closed, satin finish blade, stainless bolsters, pins and thong hole, burgundy Micarta slabs, serial #132 .... $585

HORN American Bicentennial 1776-1976 lockback, 4⅝" closed, satin finish blade, stainless bolsters and liners, brown Micarta scales, serial #13 ..... $545

HORN Bowie, 8" blade, nickel-silver pierced hilt, bolster, butt, inlay and trim on sheath, buffalo horn handle, walnut presentation case, mirror in top missing $795

HORN Baby Drop Horn lockback, 3¼" closed, nickel-silver bolster and liners, perfectly matched stag scales, #87 .... $785

HORN Baby Drop Horn lockback, 3⅜" closed, nickel-silver bolsters and liners, perfect ivory scales, #23 .... $995

HORN Baby Semi Horn lockback, 3¼" closed, nickel-silver bolsters and liners, perfectly matched stag scales, #90 .... $785

HORN Baby Semi Horn lockback, 3½" closed, nickel-silver bolsters, liners and inlay, very fine pearl scales, made for the 1979 NY show, #42 .... $725

HORN Dagger, 4¾" flat ground hand-rubbed blade, nickel-silver bolster, stag coffin handle, special Bicentennial mark, serial #002 .... $695

HORN Drop point, ⅝" blade, very tapered tang, nickel-silver bolsters, stag scales, very flat DHS, serial #1 .... $695

HORN Dropped Horn lockback, 4½" closed, nickel-silver bolsters and liners, burgundy Micarta scales, #106 .... $785

HORN Linerlock, 3⅞" closed, stainless bolsters and liners, stag scales $995

HORN Little Horn lockback, 3¼" closed, nickel-silver bolsters and liners, bone scales, #187 $695

HORN Little Horn lockback, 3¼" closed, nickel-silver bolsters, caps and liners, perfectly matched stag scales, #7 .... $985

HORN Little Horn lockback, 3¼" closed, nickel-silver bolsters and liners, perfect ivory scales, #126 .... $995

HORN Little Horn lockback, 3 11/16" nickel-silver liners, bolsters and inlay, stag scales, #148 $645

HORN Little Horn lockback, 3 11/16" closed, nickel-silver bolsters and liners, burgundy Micarta scales, #265 .... $575

HORN LHS Little Horn stiff version, hand-rubbed 2¾" flat ground 154CM blade, nickel-silver bolsters and caps, perfect ivory handle, serial #5 .... $745

HORN Lockback, 3½" closed, nickel-silver bolsters and cartridge inlay, brass liners, red jigged bone scales, marked Kansas City 1980, J HORN, serial #68 .... $745

HORN Lockback, 4" closed, ¾-size Remington, nickel-silver bolster, brass liners, red bone scales, #62 .... $895

HORN Lockback, 4" closed, ¾-size Remington, nickel-silver bolsters, brass liners, brown jigged bone scales, #152 .... $845

HORN Lockback, 4" closed, ¾-size Remington, nickel-silver bolsters, brass liners, perfectly matched stag scales, #153 .... $1095

HORN Lockback, 4" closed, nickel-silver bolsters and liners, ivory scales $895

HORN Lockback, 4⅝" closed, nickel-silver bolsters and liners, ivory scales, Indians overlooking a frontier fort hand-painted by Michael Collins on one $1,345

HORN Lockback, 4⅝" closed, nickel-silver bolsters and liners, perfect ivory scales $1,075

HORN Lockback bootknife, 4" closed, nickel-silver bolsters, engraved by Lynton McKenzie, brown jigged bone scales with silver inlay, #3 .... $1,175

HORN Lockback bootknife, 4" closed, nickel-silver bolsters, liners and inlay, perfect ivory scales, #11 .... $995

HORN Matched set of large and miniature bowies, 10¾" and 3½" blades, nickel-silver hilts, inlays, and sheath trim, stag handles, fitted sheaths, fitted red velvet-lined chest, a very early Horn set, very rare $1,395

HORN Matched skinner and caper pair, 4" blades, brass hilts, India stag scales (Redding trademark), single sheath with protective flap, 19th century style, (A buffalo hunter's set brought down to a useful size for the 20th century hunter) $795

HORN MHS StiffHorn version of MiddleHorn, 3" 154CM blade, very tapered tang, stainless bolsters and caps, ivory scales, #3 .... $695

HORN Model ¾DHL lockback, 3½" closed, nickel-silver bolsters and liners, ivory scales, crack at a pin on one side, #23 .... $595

HORN Model ¾DHL lockback, 3½" closed, nickel-silver bolsters and liners, perfectly matched stag scales, #22 .... $695

HORN Model ¾PLL, 4″ closed, ¾-size reproduction of a very rare Remington lockback, nickel-silver bolsters, liners and bullet inlay, jigged bone scales, #61 . . . . $695

HORN Model ¾RSL lockback #2, ¾-size reproduction of the Remington Lockback, 3⅜″ closed, nickel-silver bolsters, liners and bullet inlay, stag scales, this is the second numbered Remington reproduction $695

HORN Model ¾RSL lockback, 3⅜″ ¾-size reproduction of the Remington Bullet lockback, ckel-silver bolsters, liners and bullet inlay, very fine stag, #24 . . . . $695

HORN Model ¾SHL lockback, 3½″ closed, nickel-silver bolsters, liners and inlay for 79 K C show, jigged bone scales, #23 . . . . $645

HORN Model DHL lockback, 4 9/16″ closed, nickel-silver bolsters and liners, stag scales, #34 . . $745

HORN Model DHL lockback, 4 9/16″ closed, nickel-silver bolsters and liners, burgundy Micarta scales, #58 . . . . $595

HORN Model BHL Baby Horn lockback, 3⅛″ closed, nickel-silver bolsters and liners, jigged bone scales, #80 . . . . $575

HORN Model BHL Baby Horn lockback for 79 NY show, 3⅛″ closed, nickel-silver bolsters, liners and inlay, ivory scales with tiny cracks in both, #113 . . . . $455

HORN Model FBK folding lockback bootknife, 4″ closed, nickel-silver bolsters and liners, perfect ivory scales, inlay for '79 NY show, #7 . . . . . . $795

HORN Model FBK folding lockback bootknife, 4″ closed, nickel-silver bolsters and liners, ivory scales, inlay for '79 NY show, crack at a pin, one side, #11 . . . . $495

HORN Model FBK folding lockback bootknife, 4″ closed, nickel-silver bolsters and liners, ivory scales, inlay for '79 NY show, fine checks both sides, #18 . . . . $495

HORN Model PHS slipjoint, 3″ closed, nickel-silver bolsters, caps and liners, very fine pearl scales, #1, fewer than 60 made, very rare $795

HORN Model PHS slipjoint, 3″ closed, nickel-silver bolsters and liners, perfect ivory scales, #29 $645

HORN Model RSL lockback, reproduction of Remington bullet model, 4½″ closed, nickel-silver bolsters, liners and bullet inlay, stag scales, serial #8 . . . . $695

HORN Model SHL lockback, 4 9/16" closed, nickel-silver bolsters and liners, burgundy Micarta scales, #1, he original slim version that is no longer made $795

HORN Model SHLM lockback, 4 9/16" closed, nickel-silver bolsters and liners, stag scales, #20 .... $745

HORN Model SHLM lockback, 4 9/16" closed, nickel-silver bolsters and liners, green Micarta scales, #13, very rare $645

HORN Model UHL lockback, 4¼" closed, nickel-silver tbolsters and liners, stag scales, #14, rare $695

HORN Semi-skinner, 3½" 154CM blade, nickel-silver bolsters, stag scales, very tapered very slim SHSM, serial #6 .... $595

HORN Semi-skinner, 3⅜" 154CM blade, nickel-silver bolsters and caps, ivory scales, SHSM, serial #10 .... $695

HORN Semi-skinner, 3½" 154CM blade, very tapered tang, nickel-silver bolsters, ivory scales, one crack at a pin, very slim SHS, #9 .... $495

HORSE (SOLINGEN) 8¼" engraved blade, steel hilt, engraved brass wrapped finger-grooved handle with wood inlay, used, no sheath, old sword cut down $55

HOWARD Midlock, 3½" closed, 440C blade, nickel-silver bolster and fileworked liners, sheep horn scales $215

HOWIE Slipjoint, 2⅝" closed, nickel-silver fileworked liners, stainless bolsters, oosic scales, 1978 .... $80

HUBBARD, A.J. Camp, 9" blade, brass hilt and butt, India stag handle, skeleton utility knife on front of sheath, shows very little use $255

HUBBARD, A.J. Chute, 4⅝" blade, stainless steel hilt, black Micarta scales $230

HUDSON, ROBB Camp, 8" blade, tapered tang, brass pins, hardwood handle, by a master smith $335

HUDSON, ROBB Carver, 10" blade, brass bolster, fancy figured walnut handle $155

HUDSON, ROBB Hunter, 7½" satin finish blade, brass hilt and butt, fine walnut handle $395

HUESKE Dirk, 3⅞" blade, brass bolsters and butt, stag slab handle, serial #1196, no sheath $75

HUESKE Dirk, 4¾" blade, brass bolster and butt, stag slab handle, serial #1197, no sheath $95

HUESKE Drop point, 4" blade, brown Micarta handle with dark stripe, no sheath $135

HUESKE Upswept skinner, 4⅛" blade, nickel-silver hilt, butt and spacers, three-piece wood Micarta handle, #464 .... $125

HUK Drop point, 4½" blade, nickel-silver hilt, sterling trim at butt, fossilized walrus ivory handle and butt, no sheath $355

HULL, M. Spanish dagger, 9" blade, black Micarta scales, young maker shows lots of promise $165

HYER Dagger, 3" blade, all steel $45

I

I*XL 10" blade, nickel-silver hilt, stag slabs, blade pitted, no sheath $155

I*XL 10" spearpoint bowie blade, stag scales, nickel-silver trimmed sheath and knife $335

I*XL Two-blade barlow, 3⅜" closed, nickel-silver bolsters, brass liners, India stag scales, hard to open, very strong springs $40

I*XL WOSTENHOLM Three-blade Texas stock, 4⅞" closed, blade etched Texas Stock Knife, brass liners, rosewood scales $75

I*XL WOSTENHOLM (ENGLAND) Three-blade Wharncliffe stock, 4⅞" closed, Texas Stock Knife on blade, brass liners, shadow pattern rosewood scales $85

IBBERSON (SHEFFIELD ENGLAND) Three-blade swell center, 4" closed, nickel-silver bolsters, pins and inlay, brass liners, filework liners and blade back, pearl scales, used $60

IMEL 3" blade, integral stainless hilt, very tapered tang, brass pins, brown Micarta scales $235

IMEL 3¾" blade, integral hilt and butt, stainless pins, curly maple slabs $295

IMEL Drop point, 3" mirror-finish blade, full tapered tang, stainless pins, black spacers, rose-blushed ivory handle, no sheath $230

IMEL Fighter, 7¼" blade sculpted from ⅜" steel, integral hilt, subhilt and butt, fossilized oosic handles $1,295

IMEL Guthook, 3¼" blade, integral hilt, butt, stag inserts $345

IMEL Lockback, 4¼" closed, stainless frames, hippo ivory scales $435

IMEL Lockback skinner, 4" closed, stainless steel frames, pearl inserts $285

IMEL Skinner, 3¼" blade, integral hilt, butt, stag scales $365

IMEL Slipjoint, 4" closed, stainless frames, hippo ivory inserts, used $195

IMPERIAL One-blade even-end pen, 3⅛" closed, stainless bolsters and liners, celluloid scales, "Tuf-Nut" on handle, used $35

IMPERIAL Exchangeable blade knife, one stationary, three exchange blades, 2¾" closed, steel bolsters and liners, iced celluloid scales, unused but shows age $45

INDIA 9" blade, brass trim, buffalo handle, made for officers of Gurkha troops $25

INDIA Two Gurkha knives on wood plaque, stainless steel engraved butt cap and blade, horn handles, stainless emblems on plaque $75

INDIA Kukri, 12" blade, made for the British army, rosewood handle $25

INDO-PERSIAN-KURD 8" armor-piercing point blade, full tapered tang, stone handle, velvet sheath $245

INOX (FRANCE) Coffin-handled two-blade utility, 3⅛" closed, screw driver, can opener, cork screw, punch, shadow pattern jigged bone scales, sharpened and used $50

ISSARD (FRANCE) Lockback, 5¼" closed, mirror-finish blade, Kendal (a French dealer) stamped on blade, nickel-silver bolsters and pins, brass liners, stag slabs $85

J

JAMBIYA (ARAB) 8¾" curved blade $40

JAPAN Hatchet, 8½" satin-finish blade, wood handle, wood sheath $40

JAPAN WW II bayonet, 14" blade, steel hilt and butt, wood handles, steel sheath with leather frog, never used, but it is 50 years old $45

JARVENPAA (FINLAND) 3¾″ Finn blade (the puukko knife of Finland) nickel-silver bolster, butt and sheath trim, red plastic handle, very nice, at least 35 years old $45

JENKINS Miniature bowie, 3¼″ #201 steel blade, engraved brass hilt and butt, ebony handle, leather sheath, a well done miniature, very nice $155

JERNIGAN, STEVE 2⅝″ blade, filework back, brass hilt and pins, red liners, ivory Micarta slabs $150

JOHNSON, GORDON Hunter, 3¼″ blade, full tang, nickel silver pins, red liners, ivory Micarta slabs with finger grooves, serial #734 .... $85

JOHNSON, R.B. Drop point, 3½″ blade, tapered tang, brass pins and liners, hardwood scales $55

JOHNSON, RUFFIN 3⅞″ blade, stainless hilt, butt and inlay, 2-piece mesquite handle, initials on shield $295

JOHNSON, RUFFIN Clip point utility, 4¼″ blade, brass hilt and butt cap, 3-piece wood handle with brass spacers, early $130

JOHNSON, RUFFIN Fighter, 7″ blade, brass hilt, butt, sub-hilt and inlay, wood handle, engraved R.J.R., new $245

JOHNSON, S.R. 3″ 154CM blade, very tapered tang, nickel-silver hilt, burgundy Micarta scales, a very

JOHNSON, S.R. Bootknife, 3⅞″ blade, engraved nickel-silver hilt and sub hilt, burgundy Micarta scales, engraved by Henry Frank, very nice $1,345

JOHNSON, S.R. Bootknife, 4½″ mirror-finish blade, nickel-silver hilt and pins, ivory scales, outstanding work $1,295

JOHNSON, S.R. Clip point hunter, 3″ blade, hand-rubbed finish, tapered tang, nickel-silver bolsters, African blackwood slabs, new $445

JOHNSON, S.R. Ted Devlet mini-dirk, 3¼″ blade, nickel-silver bolsters, big horn sheep horn handle $695

JOHNSON, S.R. Dirk, 4″ 154CM blade, nickel-silver hilt and pins, ebony handle, Engraved by H.H. Frank $1,095

JOHNSON, S.R. Dirk, 4¼″ blade, engraved nickel-silver hilt and sub hilt, burgundy Micarta scales, engraved by Henry Frank, outstanding $1,745

JOHNSON, S.R. Dirk, 6″ dagger ATS-34 blade, nickel-silver hilt and subhilt, ivory scales, great work $1,665

JOHNSON, S.R. Drop point, 3⅝" 154CM blade, very tapered tang, nickel-silver hilt, burgundy Micarta scales $495
JOHNSON, S.R. Stiletto, 5¾" 154CM blade, very tapered tang, nickel-silver hilt and domed inlay, both sides very fine, ivory scales, rare $995
fine knife $495
JOHNSON, WILLIAM C. 3" drop point hunter, nickel-silver hilt, ivory Micarta cales $85
JU-CA Gaucho, 4¾" blade, .800 silver and gold handle and sheath, presentation box $345

K

KA-BAR Two-blade clasp, Model #V111/78, 5¼" closed, nickel-silver bolsters, caps, liners and inlay, stag scales, dog head handle inlay $145
KA-BAR Two-blade clasp, 5¼" closed, nickel-silver bolsters, caps and dog head inlay on handle, brass liners, jigged bone scales $75
KA-BAR Two-blade congress, 3⅝" closed, nickel-silver bolsters, brass liners, mother of pearl scales $65
KA-BAR Two-blade electrician's, 3⅝" closed, nickel-silver bolsters, brass liners, rosewood scales $20
KA-BAR Two-blade Jumbo Jack KaBar Club Knife, 4⅛" closed, nickel-silver bolsters and dog's head inlay, brass liners, stag scales, #10083, lightly used, box $50
KA-BAR Two-blade, serpentine, 3⅝" closed, brass liners, nickel-silver bolsters, yellow scales, pre-1940, used $40
KA-BAR Two-blade Bicentennial Commemorative trapper, 4⅛" closed, nickel-silver bolsters and caps, blue with red and white plastic scales, pouch $75
KA-BAR 4" blade, brass hilt, alloy butt, leather handle, old, may have been refinished, no sheath $30
KA-BAR Coke bottle folding hunter, Limited Edition 1981, 5¼" closed, nickel-silver bolsters and caps, brass liners and bear inlay, stag scales, serial #6459 .... $120

KA-BAR Coke bottle folding hunter, Limited Edition 1984, 5¼" closed, nickel-silver bolsters, caps and inlays, brass liners, smooth bone scales, serial #6459 .... $85

KA-BAR Fighter, 7" blade, steel hilt and butt, leather handle shortened, used, most blade coating worn off, WW II sheath shows age $40

KA-BAR Grizzly, Collector's Club Limited Edition 1986 etched blade, 5½" closed, nickel-silver bolsters and caps, brass liners, stag scales $65

KA-BAR Hobo combination—folder, fork and spoon, 3¾" closed, all steel $25

KA-BAR Dog's Head two-blade jack, 4⅛" closed, nickel-silver bolsters and inlay, brass liners, stag slabs, new, original box $75

KA-BAR KA-LOCK 1979 butt lock, 4⅛" closed, stainless bolsters, brass liners, burgundy Micarta scales $45

KA-BAR Lockback, 3½" closed, #1186 stainless blade, etched KA-BAR 7870 Knife Collectors Club, nickel-silver bolsters, brass liners, stag slabs, box $45

KA-BAR Lockback, 5" closed, brass frames, engraved India stag handle $55

KA-BAR Lockback, 5½" closed, nickel-silver rivet, brass liners $25

KA-BAR Model 1128 Wharncliffe jack, one blade and saw, 5" closed, nickel-silver bolsters, brass liners, yellow delrin scales $35

KA-BAR Model #1197 clasp, 5¼" closed, two small indentations on side of blade, nickel-silver bolsters and caps, brass liners, stag scales $35

KA-BAR Old Grizzly, 5½" closed, nickel-silver bolsters, brass liners, stag scales, excellent condition $1,255

KA-BAR Rigger, 4⅛" blade, nickel-silver hilt, wood scales, marlin spike in same sheath $20

KA-BAR WW II Survival, 6¾" blade, steel hilt and butt, leather handle, used $50

KA-BAR Swell center jack, 5¼" closed, nickel-silver bolsters, liners and inlay, stag scales, new $100

KA-BAR Unmarked 7" blade, very used good condition, USN MK 2 sheath, excellent $95

KA-BAR USMC combat, 7" blade, steel hilt, butt, leather handle, box, new $35

KA-BAR WW II combat, 7" blade, steel hilt and butt, shows little if any use and the same amount of care, USN MK 2 sheath, excellent $150

KAPELA Cap-and-ball .25 percussion pistol in in pocket knife, 4¼" closed, nickel-silver bolster, liners, ivory Micarta scales, push button, trigger $295

KAS Fighter, 7" blade, nickel-silver hilt, stainless butt, bocote handle $185

KEEN KUTTER Carver, 8½" combo knife/carving fork, stag handles, stainless trim, original box, no sheath, never used $55

KEEN KUTTER Hand ax, black blade, wood handle, unused $125

KEEN KUTTER Sleeveboard jack, 3½" closed, satin-finish blade, stainless liners, gray iced celluloid scales $35

KEEN KUTTER Swell-end jack, 3½" closed, nickel-silver shield inlay and liners, celluloid scales, carried $35

KEEN KUTTER Spirit of St. Louis three-blade premium stock, 4" closed, nickel-silver bolsters and inlay, brass liners, black delrin scales, #174, new, original box $75

KEEN KUTTER Cattleman whittler, 3¼" closed, nickel-silver bolsters and inlay, jigged bone scales, used $55

KEHIOYON, ALFREDO (HECHO A MANO) 7⅝" blade, brass hilt and pins, wood slabs, used $125

KELLEY Three-blade stock, 4" closed, brass bolsters, pins and liners, red pacawood scales $95

KEMAL Hunter, 4¾" damascus blade, steel bolster and butt, great burl wood handle, used, very good $395

KEMP Semi-skinner, 3¾" blade, nickel-silver hilt, bocote scales $115

KEMP Skinner, 3⅝" blade, stainless steel hilt and pins, ivory handle $295

KERSHAW 4½" blade, filework blade back, brass engraved hilt and butt, black delrin handle with finger grooves $95

KERSHAW Lockback, 4¾" closed, Black Horse rubber handles $45

KERSHAW 4½" blade, etched by Shaw-Liebowitz, brass hilt and butt, black nylon handle $175

KERSHAW Two-blade lockback, 3⅛" closed, stainless steel frame, wood inlay $25

KERSHAW The Bald Eagle lockback, 4" closed, brass bolsters, ivory scales with eagle scrimshaw, presentation box, 160/250 .... $245

KERSHAW Lockback, 3¼" closed, brass bolster, stainless liners, bone slabs, duck scrimshaw by G. Harbour, A & F, presentation box, 2110 .... $110

KERSHAW Lockback, 3¾" closed, brass bolsters, caps and liners, smooth bone scales $35

KERSHAW Model #1050 4¾" lockback, brass frames, black plastic scales, includes belt pouch $40

KERSHAW Model #1050 4¾" lockback, brass bolsters, pins and liners, black Micarta handle with finger grooves, leather belt sheath, used $40

KERSHAW Rotary-lock, 3⅛" closed, stainless liners, ivory Micarta scales, original box, mint $85

KERSHAW Trooper bootknife, 5⅛" blade, stainless hilt and butt, brass spacers, wood handle, #3539 .... $85

KERSHAW (GERMANY) Military bootknife, 4¾" blade, bead-blasted finish, black Micarta handle $115

KESSLER, R.A. Trailing Point Hunter Model 1, 3¼" blade, tapered tang, stainless hilt and pins, desert ironwood scales, #39, new $155

KINFOLKS Miniature, 3" blade, alloy hilt and butt, three-piece plastic handle, brass, black and coral spacers, used $40

KING Lockback, 3¾" closed, nickel-silver bolsters and liners, ivory scales, scrimshaw of walrus $175

KIOUS Two-blade pen, 2¾" closed, engraved stainless frame, inlay and liners, ivory inlay, filework blade $355

KIOUS Fighter, 6¼" blade, nickel-silver hilt and pins, super cocobolo scales $335

KIOUS Lockback, 3⅝" closed, stainless steel interframe, ebony inlays $275

KIOUS Sleeveboard, 3⅝" closed, filework on liners and blade, stainless handle with black pearl inlay $255

KIRK Hunter, 4½" blade, hand forged brass hilt and butt, rosewood handle (John Kirk is an early leader of the primitive school of knifemaking—his knives sell because of their handmade look.) $95

KISSING KRANES Four-blade congress, 3⅝" closed, brass bolsters, liners and inlay, yellow delrin scales $45

KISSING KRANES Robert Klaas eight-blade Camper, 4⅛" closed, stainless handles, very nice $115

KISSING KRANES Robert Klaas 2219XXII lockback, 4⅛" closed, nickel-silver bolster and inlay, brass liners, jigged bone scales, etching on blade worn off, used $35

KISSING KRANES R. Klaas Model #728 150-year anniversary commemorative sleeveboard, 2¾" closed, one blade engraved, nickel-silver bolsters and inlay, brass liners, jigged bone scales ... $35

KISSING KRANES R. Klaas cigar whittler, 4½" closed, nickel-silver bolsters, liners and inlay, French ivory (celluloid, an early substitute for ivory) scales, Golden Circle Knife Club 1980, 1 of 500, serial #95 .... $55

KLAAS, ROBERT Two-blade canoe, 3" closed, brass liners, nickel-silver bolsters and inlay, jigged bone scales $55

KLAAS, ROBERT Two-blade canoe, 3" closed, brass liners, nickel-silver bolsters and inlay, celluloid scales $50

KLAAS, ROBERT Bowie, 6⅛" blade etched New Orleans Bowie, brass hilt, aluminum butt, stag handle $40

KLAAS, R. (GERMANY) Love birds four-blade congress, 3⅝" closed, nickel-silver bolsters and inlay, brass liners, stag scales $65

KOLITZ, ROBERT 4½" blade hunter, cable damascus blade by George Walker, filework blade back, brass hilt and butt, stag handle, #5 ... $265

KOLLER (SOLINGEN) Bowie, 8¼" blade, brass handle and frame including hilt, blade very badly pitted $105

KRESSLER, D.F. Chute, 5" blade, integral hilt and butt, ivory scales, very fine fully-engraved tang and butt by Stanley Stoltz, the great Swedish engraver $6,400

KRESSLER, D.F. Clip point hunter, 4" rose damascus blade, brass hilt, butt, cocobolo handle, this young German maker is one of the world's finest, a rare bargain $645

KRESSLER, D.F. Clip point hunter, 5" blade, stainless hilt and pins, extremely fine stag scales, hand-rubbed $950

KRESSLER, D.F. Drop point, 3⅝" 440V PMT steel blade, perfectly matched stag scales $495

KRESSLER, D.F. Drop point, 3¼" stellite blade, nickel-silver hilt and pins, brushed Micarta handle, fantastic little Gent's Hunter by top maker, about 40% less than buying direct $485

KRESSLER, D.F. Drop point hunter, 3½" blade, integral hilt and butt, remarkable stag handle, engraved by David Perdue with scroll heavily inlaid with gold $4,600
KRUSE, MARTIN Clip point, 7" black coated blade, black carved wood handle, stainless pins, used $125

L

L F & C 1918 US Brass knuckle knife, black blade, steel handle, metal sheath $265
L F & C (USA) Two-blade jack, 3" closed, blade etched UNIVERSAL, nickel-silver bolsters, caps and inlay, stag scales $105
LAGUIOLE (FRANCE) Front bolsterlock, 4⅜" closed, fileworked brass liners, smooth horn scales $50
LAKE 4¾" A2 at 60RC blade, brass hilt and butt, exotic hardwood handle, made Jan. 1972, no sheath $295
LAKE Drop point, 3¼" hollow ground 154CM blade, nickel-silver hilt and oval escutcheons engraved by Scaggs, stag scales, no sheath, serial #7 ... $935
LAKE Gentleman's lockback, 3⅛" closed, sterling silver bolsters, liners and toothpick, super-fine pearl scales, #20, eelskin pouch $1,695
LAKE Interframe lockback, 4½" closed, aluminum body with burgundy Micarta inlay $795
LAKE Tail-lock, 2½" closed, sterling silver interframe, rhino horn inlay, ring for chain $2,135
LAKE Tail-lock, 2½" closed, sterling silver interframe, exhibition grade pearl scales, bail for watch chain $2,475
LAKE Tail-lock, 3¼" closed, sterling silver interframe, exhibition grade pearl scales, bail for watch chain, rare $2,795
LAKE Tail-lock, 4" closed, aluminum interframe, stag $1,250
LAKE Tail-lock, 4" closed, nickel-silver interframe, pearl inlays very fine $2,055
LAKE Tail-lock, 4⅜" closed, aircraft alloy interframes, rosewood inlays, serial #67 .... $895
LAKOTA Lil' Hawk, 4¾" closed, satin-finish blade, stainless bolster, wood Micarta slabs, unused $40

LAKOTA Teal lockback, 2⅝" closed, brass liners, all stainless handle, original box $30

LAMPSON Lockback, 4¾" closed, mirror-polish blade, stainless bolster and liners, wood scales, belt sheath $195

LANG, KURT 5¾" forged blade, wire-wrapped handle, chisel butt, sheath $140

LANG, KURT Camp, 7" forged blade, wire handle $125

LANG, KURT Skinner, 5⅝" blade, well-matched stag scales, what a skinner $175

LANGLEY, GENE Semi-skinner, 2⅝" blade, stainless hilt and pins, red liners, walnut scales, new $135

LARGIN, K.C. Balisong, 3⅛" closed, brass frames, wood inlays $115

LEACH Bowie, 7½" blade, stainless bolster and butt, black Micarta handle, the best Mike Leach I have seen $245

LEACH Drop point hunter, 4⅛" blade, aluminum moose horn handle scrimmed on both sides $125

LEDFORD Lockback, 3⅜" closed, nickel-silver bolsters and liners, buffalo horn scales, fileworked back $195

LEE 7" damascus blade, stainless hilt, rosewood scales $255

LEE Benchmade utility, 3½" mirror-finish blade, nickel-silver hilt and pins, black liners, nicely-matched stag slabs $125

LEE Clip point fighter, 6⅞" damascus blade, tapered tang, stainless bolsters, stag scales, no sheath $355

LEE Lockback, 4" closed, stainless bolsters, damascus blade, wood scales $175

LEE Stiletto, 4¾" damascus blade, tapered tang, stainless hilt, wood handle, no sheath $235

LEVINE, NORMAN Frontlock, 3¾" closed, stainless steel liners, bolsters and caps, very fine mother-of-pearl scales $195

LILE 3¾" closed, satin-finish blade, nickel-silver interframe, wood inlay, new $175

LILE 4" satin-finish blade, tapered tang, brass hilt, pins and thong hole, red liners, ivory Micarta slabs $205

LILE 4" satin-finish blade, tapered tang, nickel-silver pins and hilt, red liners, very nicely matched stag slabs $275

LILE 5¼" satin-finish blade, brass hilt and thong hole liner, stag handle $195

LILE 6¼" satin-finish blade, brass hilt and butt, extra fine stag handle with finger grooves $355

LILE 6½" blade, brass hilt and thong hole, red spacers, stag handle, mint $295

LILE Big 7 drop point hunter, 4" D-2 steel blade, hand-rubbed finish, brass hilt, pins and thong hole, stag slabs, red lines, new $255

LILE Bootknife, 4" satin-finish blade, tapered tang, engraved hilt and pins, wood scales, nice ... $375

LILE Bowie, 9" classic flat-ground hand-rubbed blade, nickel-silver hilt and pins, stag scales, combat sheath with diamond sharpener $785

LILE Bowie, 12" blade, brass hilt, fine walnut scales, Jimmy's big bowie and a fine one $385

LILE Chute, 4½" blade, brass hilt, ivory handles $895

LILE Custom, 2¾" mirror-finish blade, brass hilt, pins and thong hole, stag slabs $125

LILE Custom interframe buttonlock, 4¾" closed, satin-finish blade, stainless frame, oosic inlays, #457 .... $295

LILE Dagger, 6" blade, fileworked nickel-silver hilt and tang, stag scales $425

LILE Drop point, 4" blade, nickel-silver hilt and pins, India stag scales $225

LILE Drop point, 4" blade, etched in gold with a charging lion by Shaw-Liebowitz, 8/50, brass hilt, stag scales $285

LILE Featherweight drop point, 3½" blade, rosewood handle, nice little knife $140

LILE Filet, 7" blade, brass hilt, India stag handle $195

LILE Gentleman's hunter, 2¾" satin-finish blade, brass hilt and pins, stag slabs $175

LILE Hunter, 3⅞" blade, brass hilt and pins, ivory scales $265

LILE Hunter, 4" blade, very tapered tang, nickel-silver hilt, pins and thong hole, wood Micarta handle $235

LILE Interframe buttonlock, 4¾" closed, nickel-silver frames, stag inlays $345

LILE Interframe buttonlock, 4¾" closed, satin-finish D-2 steel blade, wood Micarta inlays, steel frame, #050, mint $345

LILE Interframe buttonlock, 4¾" closed, nickel-silver interframe, ivory inlays #155, mint $475

LILE Interframe lockback, 3″ closed, ivory inlays, small crack in ivory $195

LILE Lockback, 3¾″ closed, stainless bolsters and liners, surface ivory slabs, leather sheath, new $355

LILE Lockback, 4″ closed, brass liners, black Micarta scales, easy-open button $275

LILE Lockback, 4⅞″ closed, brass button on satin-finish blade, brass liners, black Micarta scales $285

LILE Rambo the Mission, 10″ sawtooth-back blade, Phillips and slot-head screwdriver hilt, stainless butt, compass in hollow cord-wrapped handle $545

LILE Rambo The Mission, 10″ sawback bead-blasted blade, steel hilt with screwdriver ends, hollow cord-wrapped handle, used, excellent .. $695

LILE Semi-skinner, 3½″ satin-finish blade, very tapered tang, nickel-silver pins, cocobolo scales with finger grooves $125

LILE Skinner, 2¾″ blade, brass hilt and pins, ivory scales $285

LILE Skinner, 2⅞″ blade, brass hilt and pins, stag scales, engraved mark on blade, early Lile $200

LILE Two-knife set, 2⅞″ blade skinner, 3⅞″ blade hunter, both blades satin-finish, brass hilts and pins, stag slabs, double sheath, extra sheath for hunter $375

LILE Upswept hunter, 7½″ blade, brass hilt and butt, finger-grooved stag handle $255

LINDER (SOLINGEN) Arizona States Line skinner, 3¾″ blade, brass hilt and pins, wood scales .. $75

LITTLE One-blade slipjoint, 3½″ closed, nickel-silver bolsters, pins and liners, ebony scales, #201 .... $175

LITTLE One-blade slipjoint, 3½″ closed, stainless bolsters and liners, wood scales, #307 ..... $195

LITTLE Lockback, 4″ closed, nickel-silver liners, bolsters and pins, ebony scales, #301 ...... $170

LITTLE Slipjoint, 3″ closed, stainless bolsters and liners, ebony scales, #251 .... $170

LITTLE Slipjoint, 4″ closed, nickel-silver frames, ebony scales $125

LITTLE Slipjoint, 4″ closed, nickel-silver bolsters, liners and pins, wood slabs, #206 .... $145

LITTLE Slipjoint, 4″ closed, nickel-silver bolsters, stag scales, serial #235 .... $195

LITTLE, BRIAN (CANADA) 6⅝″ damascus blade, hilt, butt and sheath fittings, exotic wood handle and sheath, filework hilt and blade back $535

LITTLE, GARY Camp, 6⅝″ blade, brass hilt, green Micarta handle $165

LOFGREEN (L.O.F.) Bowie, 7⅛″ blade, brass hilt and butt, stag handle $195

LOFGREEN (L.O.F.) Fighter, 7⅛″ clip point blade, brass hilt and butt, stag handle with finger grooves, early, used $195

LOFGREEN (L.O.F.) Fighter, 8″ blade, brass hilt and butt, walnut handle $275

LOFGREEN (L.O.F.) Miniature bowie, 3⅝″ blade, brass hilt and butt, ivory handle $135

LOFGREEN (L.O.F.) Slipjoint, 3″ closed, nicely engraved brass liners and bolsters, ivory Micarta handle $145

LOVELESS ST-4, 3⅝″ blade, tapered tang, nickel-silver hilt, brass pins and thong hole, coral Micarta scales, #70 of 101, new $995

LOVELESS Bootknife, 3⅝″ blade marked New York Special, nickel-silver bolster, green Micarta scales, pocket sheath, only seven of this model said to have been made $2,995

LOVELESS Bootknife, 4½″ ATS34 blade, very thin tapered tang, nickel-silver hilt, green canvas Micarta scales, shop #282 .... $1,495

LOVELESS Bootknife, 4¾″ blade, nickel-silver hilt, stag scales $1,865

LOVELESS Drop point, 3¾″ ATS34 blade, nickel-silver hilt, India stag scales, fine grooves top and bottom of handle to aid grip, shop #994, very unusual $945

LOVELESS Drop point, 4″ satin-finish ATS34 blade, no hilt, green canvas Micarta scales, half-tang model no longer made, rare $845

LOVELESS Nesmuk, 3¾″ blade, nickel-silver hilt, very well matched stag scales, #733, unusual and beautiful $1,095

LOVELESS Semi-skinner, 3⅛″ blade, small nickel-silver bolsters, very well matched stag scales, #734 .... $895

LOVELESS Semi-skinner, 3¾″ ATS34 blade, nickel-silver hilt, well-matched India stag scales ... $965

LOVELESS Straight hunter, 4″ ATS34 blade, nickel-silver hilt, India stag scales, shop # 1112, nice $945

LOVELESS Mark Lawndale fighter, 6½" blade, brass hilt, perfectly matched stag scales, stag-handled Lawndale fighters are very, very rare, no sheath $2795

LOVELESS Mark Lawndale utility, 3⅞" blade, tapered tang, nickel-silver bolsters, ivory scales with small checks, left hand sheath $1395

LOVELESS Riverside mark fighter, 5¼" blade, stainless steel hilt and pins, black Micarta handle, shop #1066, C.C.K.,JR, never used or carried ... $1495

LOVELESS Riverside mark utility hunter, 4¾" ATS34 blade, stainless steel hilt and pins, black Micarta scales, shop #1067, C.C.K., JR, new, never used or carried $845

LOVELESS-JOHNSON Dagger, 4" blade, nickel-silver hilt, ivory Micarta handle, very, very rare $2,995

LOVELESS-JOHNSON Dagger, 4¾" blade, nickel-silver hilt, ivory Micarta scales, very, very rare $2,995

LOVELESS-JOHNSON Semi-skinner, 4⅝" blade, brass hilt, burgundy Micarta scales, #764, customer's name etched on back of blade $1,995

LUDWIG, BOB Two-blade slipjoint, 3¼" closed, stainless steel liners, bolsters and caps, black Micarta scales, this early maker from Port Arthur, TX made a name for edge-holding folders before Jess Horn began to make knives, very, very rare $265

LUM Bootknife, 4⅝" satin-finish blade, tapered tang, stainless steel hilt, coral liners, stag slabs .. $395

LUM Tanto, 5⅞" satin-finish blade, tapered tang, stainless hilt, stag slabs, no sheath $655

LUM Tanto, 6½" 154CM blade, tapered tang, stainless bolsters, exotic wood scales $315

LUM Tanto, 6¾" blade, stainless bolsters, rosewood handles, no sheath $435

M

MADDOX Balisong, 4½" closed, nickel-silver liners, bolsters and caps, scrimmed ivory Micarta inserts, serial #1 .... $125

MADDOX Lockback, 3¾" closed, satin-finish blade, nickel-silver bolsters, liners, and pins, stag scales, #028 .... $225

MADDOX Slipjoint, 3⅛" closed, nickel-silver frames, burgundy Micarta scales $100

MADDOX Slipjoint, 4¼" closed, nickel-silver liners and bolsters, stag scales $125

MAINS Drop point, 3½" point, brass hilt and butt, wood handle $95

MAINS Drop point, 3½" blade, brass hilt, butt, wood Micarta handle $95

MAINS Drop point, 3½" blade, brass hilt, butt, stag handle $95

MAINS Drop point, 3½" engraved blade, Sid Bell Special, brass hilt and butt, stag handle $145

MAINS Guthook, 4" engraved blade, brass hilt and butt, stag handle $125

MACLBERRY (True Love, England) 4" skinner blade, brass hilt, stag scales $115

MANNLICHER 4" blade, integral hilt, tapered tang, stag scales $65

MAR, AL 2½" blade, brass pins and hilt, tapered tang, ivory Micarta slabs, no sheath $35

MAR, AL Bootknife, 3½" blade, brass hilt, pins and thong hole, black Micarta slabs $65

MAR, AL Bootknife, 3½" blade, brass bolsters and pins, ivory Micarta scales, includes pocket sheath $75

MAR, AL Frontlock, 3¼" closed, stainless steel bolsters, black lip, pearl scales, leather pouch $65

MAR, AL Lockback, 3¼" closed, nickel-silver bolsters, brass liners, ivory Micarta scales, carried, never sharpened $45

MAR, AL Lockback, 3¾" closed, nickel-silver bolsters, brass liners, Micarta handle $75

MAR, AL Lockback, 4⅞" closed, nickel-silver bolsters, brass liners, ivory Micarta scales, leather belt pouch, carried but not used $65

MAR, AL Lockback, 5" closed, satin-finish blade, one-hand opening button, stainless bolsters and pins, brass liners, Micarta slabs, ... $70

MAR, AL Midlock, 2⅛" closed, stainless bolsters, brass liners, abalone scales $75

MAR, AL Midlock, 4¾" closed, stainless bolsters and pins, brass liners, camouflage Micarta scales, cordura sheath, used $65

MAR, AL Midlock, 6" closed, brass liners, nickel-silver bolsters, camouflage Micarta scales, sheath $145

MAR, AL Sere I lockback, 3¾" closed, nickel-silver bolsters, brass liners, neoprene handles $65

MAR, AL Sere II lockback, 4½" closed, nickel-silver bolsters, brass liners, neoprene handles $95

MAR, AL Sere II lockback, 4½" closed, nickel-silver bolsters, brass liners, Micarta handles $95

MAR, AL (SEKI, JAPAN) Midlock, 3⅞" closed, PP162/200, stainless bolsters, brass liners and inlay, black kraton handle, used $50

MAR, AL (JAPAN) Lockback, 3½" closed, stainless bolsters, brass liners, ivory Micarta scales $40

MAR, AL (SEKI, JAPAN) Midlock, 4" closed, stainless bolsters, brass liners, ivory Micarta slabs, used $35

MANROW Slipjoint, 4" closed, inlaid into a stag crown, brass liners and bolsters, stag crown handle $165

MANROW Slipjoint, 3⅛" closed, stainless liners bolsters abalone scales $125

MANROW Slipjoint barlow, 3 1/16" closed, brass bolsters, nickel-silver liners, filework, big horn sheep scales $125

MARBLE Ideal, 4⅞" blade, brass hilt and spacers, alloy butt, leather handle, made 1947, well used, pitted blade, many years left as a user $45

MARBLE Remington-style, 6½" blade, brass hilt, aluminum butt leather handle, blade rusted and cleaned, a fine user $55

MARBLE (GLADSTONE, MI) Hunter, 6" blade, brass hilt, aluminum butt, leather handle, used $125

MARBLES Hunter, 5" blade, brass hilt and spacers, aluminum butt, India stag handle $55

MARBLES Skinner, 4" blade, brass hilt, butt cap may be horn or hard rubber, leather handle, no sheath, a user $40

MARBLES Skinner, 4½" stained and pitted blade, brass hilt, brass, red and black spacers, loose two-piece stag handle split at butt, no sheath $135

MARINGER 9½" fighter, black Micarta scales, very solidly attached (This young maker is both talented and well trained, his front-opening Kydex shoulder sheath is really great) $375

MARTTINI, J. 4⅜" blade, nickel-silver hilt and butt, wood handle, engraved blade, used $25

MAYHALL Two-blade jack, 4" closed, nickel-silver bolster, brass liners, stag scales, unused but sharpened $140

McALPIN Bowie, 8⅝" flat ground hand-rubbed filework-back blade, nickel-silver reinforced hilt, ebony handle, #28 .... $535

McALPIN Bowie, 8⅝" flat ground, hand-rubbed blade, nickel-silver hilt, inlays, ivory scales #30 ..... $535

McBURNETT Bootknife, 4¾" blade, nickel-silver bolster, rosewood handle, very early work by a rare talent who now specializes in folders, from Sid Latham collection $245

McBURNETT Frontlock, 3⅝" closed, nickel-silver bolsters and inlay, filework on liners and spine, fossilized oosic scales $375

McBURNETT Frontlock, 3⅝" closed, engraved nickel-silver bolsters, fileworked liners, brown jigged bone scales $485

McBURNETT Frontlock, 3¾" closed, nickel-silver liners and bolsters, fileworked liners, cattle horn scales $295

McBURNETT Frontlock, 4" closed, engraved nickel-silver bolsters, fileworked liners, green bone scales $475

McBURNETT Frontlock, 4½" closed, one-hand opening button, engraved nickel-silver bolsters and caps, fileworked liners, ironwood scales with inlay $795

McBURNETT Frontlock, 4½" closed, engraved nickel-silver bolsters and caps, fileworked liners, ivory scales with scrimmed big horn sheep $845

McBURNETT Frontlock, 4⅝" closed, nickel-silver frames, fileworked bolsters, engraved ivory scales, gold inlay one side, scrimmed the other, crack at pin on back $250

McBURNETT Frontlock, 5¼" closed, engraved nickel-silver bolsters, caps and inlay, fileworked liners and spine, the finest pink ivory I have ever seen, super work $995

McBURNETT Frontlock fighter, 5¼" closed, one-hand opening button, engraved nickel-silver bolsters and caps, fileworked liners and spine, ebony scales inlaid with shield and with ivory dice—7 one side, 11 the other $795

McBURNETT Frontlock fighter, 5½" closed, one-hand opening button, engraved nickel-silver bolsters and caps, fileworked liners and spine, silver wire inlaid maple handles, Harvey McBurnett's engraving has really come of age, he's very good $995

McBURNETT Frontlock fighter, 5¾" closed, one-hand opening button, engraved nickel-silver bolsters and caps, fileworked spine and liners, silver wire inlaid maple handles $895

McBURNETT Midlock, 3 5/16" closed, nickel-silver inlay and engraved bolsters, filework liners, ivory scales, leather pouch $495

McBURNETT Midlock, 3⅝" closed, nickel-silver bolsters, pins and inlay, filework liners, rosewood scales $295

McBURNETT Midlock, 4" closed, mirror-finish blade, engraved nickel-silver bolster and inlay, filework liners, cocobolo scales $675

McBURNETT Midlock, 4" closed, engraved nickel-silver bolsters and filework liners, smooth stag scales, D-2 steel, mint $455

McBURNETT Midlock, 4⅝" closed, nickel-silver bolsters, filework liners and blade, cocobolo scales with skull crusher $365

McBURNETT Slipjoint, 3⅝" closed, nickel-silver bolsters, filework liners, smooth sheep horn scales $295

McCARTY Bowie, 8⅛ spearpoint blade, nickel-silver hilt, subhilt and butt, black Micarta scales ... $255

McCARTY Bowie fighter, 7¾" blade, nickel-silver hilt and subhilt, stainless butt, black Micarta scales $265

McCARTY Drop point, 3½" blade, brass hilt, tulip wood scales $105

McCARTY Hunter's bowie, 4⅝" blade, nickel-silver hilt, stag scales $160

McCARTY, Z. Butterfly, 6" closed, drop point blade, all stainless steel, sheath $295

McCARTY Clip point, 4⅜" blade, nickel-silver hilt, cocobolo scales $105

McCARTY, Z. Drop point skinner, 4" blade, brass hilt, black paper base Micarta, early work, used ... $75

McCARTY, Z. Hunter, 5⅛" damascus blade, brass hilt, leather and crown stag handle $195

McCORMICK, J. Push dagger, 2½" blade, wood handle, brass pins $35

McDERMOT Semi-skinner, 4" hollow-ground mirror-polish blade, full tang, coral liners, brass hilt and butt, yellow Micarta scales $75

MEIER Skinner, 4" damascus blade by one of the pioneers of modern damascus, sterling silver bolster and butt, ivory scales, zipper case, no sheath $445

MEIER, D. Arkansas toothpick, outstanding 6½" damascus blade, sterling silver hilt, butt and sheath, ivory handle is one of the most beautiful pieces of ivory that I have ever seen $1,345

MEIER-TERZUOLA Viking dagger, 9" damascus blade by D. Meier, handle carved of solid jade by Bob Terzuola, no sheath, zipper case, very nice indeed $1,535

MILLER Drop point hunter, 4" blade, wood scales, stainless pins, tapered tang, mirror-finish, new, nice grind $85

MILLER Fighter, 5½" blade, stainless hilt, ivory Micarta scales $125

MILLER, H.J. Moran-style camp, 11" forged high-carbon steel mirror-finish blade, nickel-silver hilt and pins, cocobolo handle, wood lined sheath ... $395

MILLER, J.P. 4½" uniquely forged blade so the tang is 1/3 thinner at the handle $135

MILLER, J.P. 5¼" filework-back blade forged so the tang is 1/3 thinner at the handle $145

MILLER, TED The knife as native American art, brass hilt, ram's head carved stag handle inlaid with turquoise, wall-hanging walnut display frame ... $295

MIMS, JOHN Bootknife, 4⅛" blade, brass hilt, butt and shield, black Micarta handle, John was an outstanding 1960s maker, made very few knives before his death, all very nice $135

MINNICK SHAW-LIEBOWITZ Push dagger, 3¾" blade, cast sterling silver handle with gold ram one side, gold banner other, #17/300, plush presentation box $255

MOEDE (SOLINGEN) Multi-blade senator, 3⅝" closed, stainless blades, brass liners, cattle horn scales $155

MOEDE (SOLINGEN) Multi-blade senator, 3⅝" closed, stainless steel blades, brass liners, India stag scales $175

MOELLER 4⅜" blade, black cover with bright high-lights, the best-looking thrower I have seen .. $125

MORAN Bodkin, 4 5/16" blade, brass handles, unmarked, belt sheath $275

MORAN Bodkin, 4 5/16" blade, brass handles, unmarked, belt sheath $345

MORAN Bodkin, 4 5/16" blade, brass handles, unmarked, pocket or purse sheath $275

MORAN Clip point patch, 3⅝" blade ground flat one side for a right handed shooter to cut away from himself, brass bolster and bullet starter, fiddle back maple $795

MORAN Dagger, 5½" blade, 35" belt with steel sheath curved to fit body and copper buckle decorated with ivory-handled bowie, sheath in belt is very rare $1,125

MORAN Fighter, 8" blade, brass hilt and butt, rosewood handle, Limekiln Trademark, We get one of these only about every 10 years $2,795

MORAN Skinner, 6⅜" closed Skinner blade, brass hilt and butt, rosewood handle, Limekiln Trademark $825

MORAN Skinner, 6⅜" blade, brass hilt and butt, rosewood handle Limekiln trademark $895

MORGAN Dagger, 5½" 440C blade, nickel-silver hilt, red liners, ivory Micarta slabs, serial #385 .... $110

MORGAN Dagger, 5⅞" filework back 440C blade, nickel-silver subhilt and thong hole, red liners, black Micarta slabs, serial #986 .... $150

MORGAN Drop point, 3½" 440C blade, brass pins, tan Micarta slabs $65

MORGAN, JEFF Semi-skinner, 3" 440C blade, nickel-silver pins, ivory Micarta slabs $85

MORGAN, JEFF Small game, 3" 440C blade, burgundy Micarta scales, very promising work $80

MORGAN, TOM Camp, 7" blade, pacawood handle, remarkable work for the price $75

MORGAN, TOM Hunter, 3½" blade, brown and tan Micarta scales, a small user $55

MORGAN, TOM Tomahawk, brass head, maple handle, many inlays $150

MORGAN, TOM Tomahawk, steel head, maple handle, many brass inlays $150

MORRIS, C.H. Linerlock, 4¾" closed, stainless bolsters and liners, ironwood scales $315

MORSETH, HARRY Note: Harry's shop knives were made by him and kept on his work bench until his death. I bought them in 1971 along with the Morseth operation. Bone handles with copper pins. Of particular interest to anyone who collects Morseth knives or who specializes in early 20th century knifemakers like Morseth, Scagle or others. See page 93.

MORSETH, HARRY 4¼" laminated steel blade, brass hilt, rosewood handle, no sheath, made in the early 50s, (may be a prototype Michigan Sportsman) $195

MORSETH, HARRY 4¾" laminated steel blade, nickel-silver hilt, leather handle, black butt, no sheath, made in the early 60s $145

MORSETH, HARRY 5½" laminated steel blade made about 1950-55, nickel-silver hilt, ebony handle, no sheath used, unusual $175

MORSETH, HARRY 5¾" laminated steel blade made between 1967 and 1970, nickel-silver hilt, teak handle, no sheath $155

MORSETH, HARRY 6" laminated steel blade, brass hilt, stag handle made before 1952, (may be a prototype from much earlier), no sheath $220

MORSETH, HARRY Alaskan Hunter, 4¾" blade, nickel-silver hilt, three-piece stag handle, red, white and black spacers, used $175

MORSETH, HARRY Bootknife, 3½" blade, nickel-silver hilt, alloy butt cap, coral Rucarta handle, made from original Morseth Brusletto blade, early 70's, only 24 made $145

MORSETH, HARRY Bootknife, 4" long, nickel-silver hilt, yellow Micarta handle, made about 1972, never used $150

MORSETH, HARRY Bootknife, 4¼" blade, nickel-silver hilt, burgundy Micarta handle, no sheath, unused $275

MORSETH, HARRY Bowie, 6⅞" blade, nickel-silver double-lugged hilt, alloy butt cap, black Micarta handle $295

MORSETH, HARRY Brusletto, lightly-rusted 6" laminated steel blade, nickel-silver hilt, teakwood handle, Safe-Lok sheath, 1950s, never used or sharpened $295

MORSETH, HARRY Clip point, 4⅝" laminated steel blade, nickel-silver hilt and butt cap, three-piece stag handle $175

MORSETH, HARRY Clip point, 5⅞" blade, nickel-silver hilt, teak handle, original Safe-Lok sheath $325

MORSETH, HARRY Clip point, 6" 440C laminated steel blade, nickel-silver hilt, two-piece stag handle, lined Safe-Lok sheath $365

MORSETH, HARRY Dagger, 4" blade, nickel-silver hilt, brass butt, black Micarta handle, prototype made in the early 1970s but never put into production $185

MORSETH, HARRY Drop point, 3" laminated steel blade, nickel-silver hilt, leather handle with black butt, no sheath, made in 1971 and kept in shop ... $145

MORSETH, HARRY Drop point, 3½" laminated steel blade, nickel-silver hilt, 3-piece stag handle, not as fine as our current makers' work $155

MORSETH, HARRY Drop point hunter, 4½" 440C satin-finish laminated steel blade, nickel-silver hilt, three-piece India stag handle, 1989, new $205

MORSETH, HARRY Drop point kit, 3½" laminated steel blade, nickel-silver hilt, India stag handle, very nice $150

MORSETH, HARRY Lockback, 3⅝" closed, alloy frames, black Micarta handles, fine, rare $245

MORSETH, HARRY Lockback, 3⅝" closed, alloy frames, burgundy Micarta scales, very fine, very rare $245

MORSETH, HARRY Lockback, 4⅛" closed, alloy frames, black Micarta scales (these have not been made for years, very rare, very desirable) $245

MORSETH, HARRY Lockback, 4¼" closed, laminated steel blade, alloy frame, black Micarta scales $245

MORSETH, HARRY Lockback, 5⅛" closed, coral Rucarta handles, no liners, only 3 of these made with laminated blade $235

MORSETH, HARRY Model 1, 3½" laminated steel blade, nickel-silver hilt, red, white and black spacers, cocobolo handle, lightly used $185

MORSETH, HARRY Model 2, 4" clip point satin-finish blade, nickel-silver hilt, cocobolo handle, new, made prior to 1988, strange sheath $95

MORSETH, HARRY Model 4 Cascade Skinner, 4¼" laminated steel hollow-ground blade, nickel-silver hilt, stag handle $205

MORSETH, HARRY Model 5, 5¾" satin-finish laminated steel blade, stainless hilt, cocobolo scales, used, not original sheath $175

MORSETH, HARRY Model 6, 6" laminated steel blade, nickel-silver hilt, stag handle, made in Clinton, WA in 1969-71, lined sheath, mint $395

MORSETH, HARRY Model 7 1988 Fighter, 7" clip point blade, nickel-silver hilt, sub-hilt and butt, new stag handles done by Tom Sigmon, a bright young maker $355

MORSETH, HARRY Model 9 Pilot-Parachute, 4⅝" blade, stainless hilt, aluminum butt, burgundy Micarta handle, used $255

MORSETH, HARRY Model 9 Parachute Pilot-Survival, 4¾" laminated steel blade, nickel-silver hilt and thong hole, burgundy Micarta handle, black and white spacers $295

MORSETH, HARRY Modified bowie, 5⅞" blade, nickel-silver hilt, leather and stag handle, original Safe-Lok sheath $435

MORSETH, HARRY Parachute, 4¾" laminated steel blade, nickel-silver hilt, three-piece stag handle, not as good as our current makers' work, cuts just fine $175

MORSETH, HARRY Semi-skinner, 3¼" laminated steel blade, nickel-silver bolster, alloy butt, wood Micarta handle $175

MORSETH, HARRY Shop knife made from laminated steel and signed, 4⅜" blade, bone handles, copper pins, no sheath. See page 90 .... $165

MORSETH, HARRY Skinner, 4" laminated steel blade, nickel-silver hilt, famous 3-piece stag handle, very fine, made in 1973 .... $195

MORSETH, HARRY Skinner, 4" laminated steel (tool steel center core at 64 Rockwell, soft iron on sides) blade, nickel-silver hilt, famous 3-piece stag handle, made between 1967-71, very rare save-lock sheath with fiber liner $375

MORSETH, HARRY Skinner, 4" pitted laminated steel blade, nickel-silver hilt, wood Rucarta handle $105

MORSETH, HARRY Skinner, 4⅛" blade, nickel-silver hilt, alloy butt cap, three-piece stag handle, stamped, not etched, about 10 years old, never used ... $255

MORSETH, HARRY Skinner, 4¼" laminated steel blade, nickel-silver hilt, leather handle with black butt, made in 1967 and kept in shop, no sheath ... $175

MORSETH, HARRY Skinner, 4¼" blade, nickel-silver hilt, famous three-piece stag handle, Safe-Lok sheath $365

MUELA (SPAIN) Commando, 6¼" blade steel hilt, black plastic handle and sheath, new $25

MULLIN, STEVE Midlock, 3¾" closed, 154CM blade, stainless bolsters and filework liners, very nice Ivory slabs $325

MURPHY, DAVE Bowie, 9¼" blade, brass hilt and butt, myrtle wood handle $230

MURPHY Combat Vietnam Marine Commemorative, 6" clip point bowie blade, ornate brass hilt and butt cap, leather handle with marine insignia, gold etched In Honor of the U.S. Marines—Vietnam on blade, wood display box with camouflage liner, authenticity papers, no sheath $225

MURPHY, DAVE Hunter, 4¾" blade, aluminum handle frame, exotic wood inlays $95

MURPHY, DAVE Hunter, 5½" blade, aluminum frame, exotic wood inlays used $95

MUTH, W.H., II Slipjoint, satin-finish blade, 4½" closed, nickel-silver bolsters and liners, stag slabs, nice $175

MYERS Slipjoint, 2⅝" closed, fancy stainless handles, copper inlays and filework, new $265

N

NCCO One-blade women's-leg-and-shoe slipjoint, 5" closed, nickel-silver bolsters, brass liners, red and yellow plastic scales $25

NKCA Club knives, 1975 to 1983, all nine in padded case, all nice $765

NKCA Two-blade even end, 4¼" closed, blade etched 1981, nickel-silver bolsters, brass liners, stag scales $55

NKCA-CASE Lockback hunter, 5⅜" closed, blade etched 1983, folding hilt, nickel-silver bolsters and caps, brass liners, jigged bone scales, #3351 $125

NKCA-CASE Swell-center jack, 5⅜" closed, blade etched NKCA 1983, nickel-silver bolsters and inlay, brass liners, pacawood scales, #5969 of 6000, hard to unlock $120

NKCA-CASE Single-blade trapper, 4⅛" closed, blade etched 1979, nickel-silver bolsters and liners, stag scales $65

NKCA-CASE Trapper, 4 4/8" closed, blade etched 1985, nickel-silver bolsters and caps, brass liners, green jigged bone scales $65

NKCA-GERBER Lockback, 3⅝" closed, blade etched 1986, nickel-silver bolster and liners, jigged bone scales, serial #2830 of 6200 .... $75

NKCA-KISSING KRANE Gunstock cattle, 4" closed, blade etched 1980, nickel-silver bolsters, brass liners, stag scales $75

NKCA-KISSING KRANE Cattle, 4¼" closed, blade etched 1977, nickel-silver bolsters, brass liners, stag scales $85

NKCA-KISSING KRANE Lockback, 4¼", blade etched Hen & Rooster 1984, nickel-silver bolsters and caps, brass liners, jigged bone scales ... $75

NKCA-SCHRADE Two-blade trapper, 3¾" closed, blade etched 1982, nickel-silver bolsters and caps, brass liners, stag scales $45

NOGENT (FRANCE) Utility, 3⅛" closed, spear-point blade, can opener, cork screw, shadow pattern stainless liners and shackle, lovely ox horn cales $65

NOLEN, JIM Belt buckle knife clipped on small belt, copper trim on buckle, nickel-silver clip holds knife, stag scales $145

NOLEN Belt buckle knife, 2¾" blade, stag scale $130

NOLEN, JIM Small dagger across front of belt buckle, copper and nickel-silver on buckle, yellow Micarta handle with red lines $140

NOLEN Drop point, 4" fileworked blade, brass bolster and butt, Kudu horn handle, #8 African Series $195

NOLEN, JIM Drop point caper, 3⅛" blade, fileworked spine, oosic scales, sharpened, nice little knife $115

NOLEN Balisong, 4½" closed, filework blade back, nickel-silver bolsters and liners, bone scales $220

NOLEN Drop point skinner, 4½" filework blade, brass pins, wood slab finger-groove handle $165

NOLEN Guthook, 4" fileworked blade, brass hilt and butt, gemsbok horn handle, #1 Gemsbok African Series $265

NOLEN Skinner, 4½" guthook blade, brass hilt and spacers, pacawood handle, no sheath $75

NORTH AFRICAN Arm Dagger, 7" blade, leather and snake skin handle and sheath $165

NORWAY Fish, 2¾" blade, brass hilt, fish head handle, fish body sheath $50

O

OAXGA 9" engraved stainless blade, engraved horn handle, horse head butt, lions on hilt, lightly used $25

OCHS, CHARLES 4⅛" blade, brass hilt and pins, fantastic quality stag handle $195

OGG Folding hunter, 4¾" closed, nickel-silver bolsters and liners, ivory scales, #1372 . . . . $175

OGG Slipjoint, nickel-silver bolsters and liners, zebra wood scales $175

OGG Slipjoint, 3" closed, brass liners, nickel-silver bolsters, serial #1001, ivory scales scrimmed by Adam Funmaker $275

OGG Slipjoint, 3" closed, brass liners, nickel-silver bolsters, black Micarta $230

OGG One-blade slipjoint, 3¼" closed, nickel-silver bolsters and liners, ivory Micarta slabs $135

OGG 3¾" slipjoint, nickel-silver bolsters and liners, African Blackwood scales, checkered $195

OGG Slipjoint, 3¾" closed, brass liners, nickel-silver bolsters, serial # 1000, ivory scales with Geronimo scrimmed by Adam Funmaker $285

OGG Slipjoint, 3⅞" closed, brass liners and bolsters, walnut scales $175

OGG Slipjoint, 4½" closed, nickel-silver liners and bolsters, stag scales #1630 .... $225

OGG Slipjoint, 4¾" closed, brass bolsters and liners, green Micarta scales, fire starter inlaid in scale, striker on chain, very rare $215

OGG Slipjoint, 4¾" closed, nickel-silver bolsters, brass liners, ebony scales #1453 .... $220

OLBERTZ, FRIEDRICH (SOLINGEN) Three-blade stock, 3⅞" closed, nickel-silver bolsters and shield inlay, brass liners, brown jigged bone scales, new, original box $40

OLBERTZ, R. (GERMANY) Premium stock, 3¾" closed, blade etched Premium Stock Knife, toothpick and tweezers, nickel-silver inlay, brass liners, black vulcanized fiber scales $75

OLESON California bowie, 5" blade, nickel-silver sheath, hilt and wrapped handle with abalone inlay $425

OLSEN Camp, 7" blade, brass hilt, stag scales, used $135

OLSEN Upswept skinner, 3⅝" satin-finish blade, brass hilt, wood Micarta slabs $45

OLSON, LEE, JR. 3¾" mirror-finish blade, full tang, brass pins, wood slabs, no sheath $45

OLSON, LEE, JR., 5½" blade, brass pins, wood slabs, new $55

OLSEN KNIFE CO. Sleeveboard lockback jack, 6" closed, nickel-silver bolsters, brass liners, jigged bone scales, shows age $175

OLSEN KNIFE CO. Skinner, 3" blade, brass hilt, aluminum butt, stag handle, sheath cut $40

OLSEN Upswept skinner, 4" blade, brass pins, wood slabs, full tang, no sheath $30

ONTARIO KNIFE U.S. Air Force survival, 5" blade, steel hilt and butt, leather handle $20

OUTFITTER Bowie, 6¼" blade, steel hilt, wood Micarta scales $100

OUTFITTER Kukri, 8½" blade, black Micarta handles, early version of Vought's kukri, may be prototype $135

OUTFITTER Kukri, 9" blade, Micarta handle, bead-blasted, shows some handling but little use $125

OVEREYNDER, T.R. 1986 Midlock, 3⅝" closed, 154CM blade, stainless pins and liners, black and gold Micarta slabs, very slim $335
OX Fighter, 7⅝" blade, steel hilt and butt cap, stag handles, blade scratched $275

P

PACIFIC CUTLERY 3½" blade, black Micarta handle $25
PACIFIC CUTLERY 3¾" blade, black handles $35
PACIFIC CUTLERY 4" blade, burgundy Micarta scales, only mark Samson with Lion $35
PACIFIC CUTLERY Balisong custom bowie butterfly, 5⅛" closed, stainless steel, black Micarta scales, belt sheath, original box, new $275
PACIFIC CUTLERY Balisong butterfly, 5" closed, mariner style blade, all stainless steel, original box, new, rare $295
PACIFIC CUTLERY Balisong butterfly, 5⅛" closed, clip bowie blade, all stainless $275
PACIFIC CUTLERY Balisong butterfly, 5⅛" closed, bead blasted tanto blade and bolsters, black Micarta scales, sheath, original box, new $295
PACIFIC CUTLERY Butterfly, 4¼" closed, drop point blade, all stainless, sheath $40
PACIFIC CUTLERY Barry Wood butterfly, 3⅝" closed, stainless handles, first version, only 1,200 made $60
PACIFIC CUTLERY Caper, 2" blade, black handles $25
PACIFIC CUTLERY Fer de Lance self-hilt, 6¼" blade, black Micarta scales, bead blasted ... $125
PACIFIC CUTLERY Lockback, 4" closed, stainless bolster camouflage Micarta handle $65
PACIFIC CUTLERY Samson Series lockback, 4" closed nickel-silver bolster, black Micarta scales $40
PACIFIC CUTLERY Samson Series lockback, 5" closed nickel-silver bolsters, black Micarta scales $40
PAL CUTLERY CO. Letter opener, 5½" blade, pen knife in handle, celluloid scales $35

PAL CUTLERY CO. Letter opener, 5⅝" blade, 2¼" closed pocket knife in yellow iced celluloid handle, Rock Ola Dist. by H & H Music Co., no sheath $30

PARAPLUIE AL'EPREUVE (FRANCE) Utility, 4⅛" closed, two spear point blades, screwdriver, can opener, corkscrew and punch, embossed brass scales $40

PARDUE Clip point fighter, 7⅜" satin-finish blade, tapered tang, stainless hilt, pins and thong hole, brown Micarta scales, no sheath, 11-77, new $245

PARDUE Lockback spearpoint bowie, 5¾" closed, nickel-silver liners and bolsters, exhibition grade pearl, #24 .... $285

PARDUE Coffin-handled lockback, 4½" closed, nickel-silver bolsters liners and caps, exhibition grade pearl, #40 .... $235

PARDUE Linerlock, 5¼" closed, stainless steel bolster, skull crusher, ironwood scales $255

PARDUE Left-handed linerlock, 5 7/16" closed, stainless steel bolster and blade, kudu horn scales, first left-handed linerlock made $525

PARDUE Lockback, 3½" closed, nickel-silver bolsters and liners, stag scales, #34 .... $295

PARDUE Lockback, 4½" closed, satin-finish blade, stainless bolster and liners, horn scales, new $385

PARDUE Lockback, 4¾" closed, nickel-silver bolsters and filework liners, ironwood scales, carried and sharpened, #24 .... $135

PARDUE Lockback bootknife, 4⅝" closed, satin-finish blade, nickel-silver bolsters and liners, ivory Micarta scales, #006 .... $265

PARDUE Lockback dagger, 5¾" closed, nickel-silver liners, bolsters and caps, exhibition grade pearl scales, lots of green and pink, #24-D $265

PARDUE Lockback skinner, 4" closed, nickel-silver liners and bolsters, surface cape buffalo horn, serial #26 .... $230

PARDUE Lockback skinner, 4⅛" closed, nickel-silver bolsters and liners, ivory Micarta handles #13 .... $195

PARDUE, MEL/SCHWARZER, STEVE Lockback, 4⅝" closed, damascus blade, nickel-silver bolsters, ivory scales, engraved by Fred Harrington $485

PARKER Jack, 5¼" closed, blade etched Eagle Brand Cutlery, nickel-silver bolsters, brass liners, bone scales $40

PARKER Gypsy Butterfly, 5" closed, satin-finish surgical steel blade, brass engraved handle and liners, original box new $25

PARKER Two-blade swell center jack, 5¼" closed, bear etched blade, nickel-silver bolsters, brass liners, bone scales $40

PARKER Coffin-handled slipjoint, 3" closed, file-worked backspring and blade, nickel-silver bolsters and caps, abalone scales $35

PARKER Tanto, 6" blade, rayskin handle, blue wrap, silver and gold metal handle trim, leather-covered wood sheath $50

PARKER Tanto, 8" blade, rayskin handle, brown wrap and gold color metal fittings, leather-covered wood sheath $50

PARKER (JAPAN) blade etched LIBERTY, ornate nickel-silver bolsters and caps, brass liners jigged bone scales, serial #084 .... $90

PARKER (JAPAN) Lockback, 6¼" closed, blade etched NEVER FAIL, nickel-silver bolsters and caps, brass liners, second-cut stag scales, serial #099 $70

PARKER BROTHERS Dagger, 3¼" blade, die cast zinc handle $15

PARKER BROTHERS Two-blade lockback, both lock, 4½" closed, etched blade, nickel-silver bolsters, brass liners, bone slabs $45

PARKER CUTLERY CO. Bootknife dagger, 4¾" blade, all steel, used $15

PARKER-EDWARDS Two-blade jack, 4⅛" closed, damascus blades, nickel-silver bolsters, brass liners, jigged bone scales $35

PARKER-EDWARDS Lockback, 4⅛" closed, damascus blade, nickel-silver bolsters, brass liners, bone scales, leather belt sheath $45

PARKER CUTLERY CO. Lockback, 4⅜" closed, damascus blade nickel-silver bolsters, brass liners, stag scales $45

PARKER-EDWARDS ABC Limited Edition 1985 lockback, 5" closed damascus blade, nickel-silver bolsters, brass liners, stag scales $45

PARKER-EDWARDS American Blade Collectors 1985 lockback, 4⅞" closed, damascus steel blade, nickel-silver bolsters and caps, brass liners, second-cut stag scales, #602 .... $45

PARKER-EDWARDS American Blade Collection 1985 lockback, 5" closed, damascus blade, nickel-silver bolsters, brass liners stag scales, #663 of 5000 .... $45

PARKER-EDWARDS American blade lockback, 5" closed, nickel-silver bolsters and caps, brass liners, second-cut stag scales, serial #1220 of 5000 $50

PARKER-EDWARDS American Blade Collectors 1985 lockback, 4⅞" closed, damascus blade, nickel-silver bolsters and caps brass liners, second-cut stag scales, serial #1656 .... $45

PARKER-EDWARDS Limited edition 1985 ABC lockback, 5" closed, damascus blade, brass liners, nickel-silver bolsters, stag scales, serial #1688, new $65

PARKER-EDWARDS ABC 5th year survival, 10" Alabama-made damascus steel blade, steel hilt, checkered metal handle, butt compass, serial #100 .... $195

PARKER-EDWARDS Trapper, 4⅛" closed, two damascus blades, nickel-silver bolsters and caps, brass liners, second-cut stag scales $40

PARKER-FROST One-blade sleeveboard jack, 3⅞" closed, blade etched Little Bandit, nickel-silver bolsters, brass liners, red jigged bone scales, #28 $60

PARKER-FROST Two blade trapper, 3⅞" closed, nickel-silver bolsters, brass liners, red jigged bone scales $45

PARRISH (HASTINGS KNIFE WORKS) Camp, 9" blade, nickel-silver hilt and butt, rosewood handle $270

PARRISH (R.P. KNIVES) Fighter, 7¾" bead-blasted blade, black Micarta handle $145

PARRISH, R. Survival, 6" sawtooth-back bead-blasted blade, hilt and butt, hollow black rubber handle, compass $175

PARRISH, ROBERT 6" sawtooth-back bead-blasted blade, cord handle used $135

PASS Bootknife, 4 ½" blade, ivory Micarta scales $295

PASS Bowie, 9¼" filework flat-ground hand-rubbed blade, nickel-silver hilt, stag scales, no sheath $355

PAUL Mariner's buttonlock, 4½" closed, bead-blasted frame, ivory Micarta onlays, serial #8 $895

PASS Caper, 3½" blade, improved stag handles $175

PASS Drop point, 4" blade, very tapered tang, stainless pins ivory Micarta scales $155

PASS Drop point, 4" flat-ground hand-rubbed point 154CM blade, nickel-silver hilt, stag scales, very nice $265

PASS Fighter, 5½" blade, nickel-silver hilt, ivory Micarta scales $255

PAUL 4⅛" closed, stainless steel blade and handle, in pouch and original canister, new, very, very rare $1,195

PAUL 4½" closed, stainless steel blade and handle, serial #5 .... $995

PAUL POEHLMANN Buttonlock, 4½" closed, ivory Micarta onlays, #24, leather pouch $895

PCD Drop point, 3¼" mirror-finish blade, very tapered tang, nickel-silver hilt, pins and thong hole, black liners, wood slabs $95

PCD Gent's, 3" mirror-finish blade, brass pins, nickel-silver butt, cap, black liners, stag slabs $85

PEASE Bootknife, 3" blade, nickel-silver filework bolsters, fossilized oosic scales $255

PEASE Bootknife, 3⅜" blade, nickel-silver bolsters and butt, India stag scales $220

PEASE Lockback bootknife, 4½" closed, aircraft alloy frame, very fine pearl scales $355

PEASE Mini bootknife, 2¾" blade, nickel-silver hilt, Micarta scales, no sheath $175

PEASE Lockback, 4 5/16" closed, stainless bolsters, oosic scales $320

PEASE Lockback, 4⅝" closed, stainless steel bolster, filework liners, big horn handles, engraved ram's head by FAH, mint $795

PEASE Midlock, 5" closed, stainless bolsters, stag handles, #02SM20 .... $535

PENDLETON Drop point #7 made in 1979, 2½" blade, very tapered tang, nickel-silver hilt, hippo ivory scales $125

PENDLETON Drop point hunter, 4" blade, nickel-silver hilt, yellow Micarta scales, unused but at least 8 years old, very fine work, shopworn $145

PENDLETON Hunter, 3⅜" 154CM blade, nickel-silver bolster, black Micarta scale $135

PENDRAY Bowie, 11" blade, nickel-silver hilt, rosewood handle, swivel sheath, Al Pendray is a top smith and one of the developers of modern wootz steel, he is one of the few men I would go to for a forged blade $345

PEPPER Skinner, 4¼" blade, brass hilt, ivory Micarta scales $75

PERSIAN 10" blade, brass and german silver $50

PERSIAN Antique Persian or Indian 500-1000 year-old Wootz 6¾" blade, original gold overlay at base of tang still intact, cloisonne handle probably less than 100 years old, no sheath, zipper case $1,345

PETERSON, DAN L. Fighter, 8" damascus steel blade, stainless steel hilt and butt, African black-wood handle, waistband sheath with stud .. $285

PETERSON, E.G. Drop point, 4⅜" ATS-34 steel blade, stainless interframe, ironwood inlays $195

PETERSON, E.G. Lockback, 4" closed, stainless bolsters and liners, ironwood scales, rat-tail sheath $230

PETERSON, E.G. Lockback, 4⅞" closed, nickel-silver bolsters and liners, stag scales, belt pouch $335

PHILIPPINES Butterfly, 5¾" closed, stainless steel blade, brass liners and bolsters, bone scales, no sheath $45

POKER & LIVE (SHEFFIELD) Dagger, 7½" blade marked Gambler's Companion, nickel-silver hilt, ivory scales, patina over all, a very fine old knife $250

POLK Slipjoint, 3½" closed, nickel-silver bolsters, caps and liners, stag scales, nice $145

POP Drop point, 3½" blade, stainless hilt, ivory Micarta scales, no sheath $145

POP Drop point, 3" blade, stainless steel hilt, wood Micarta scales $155

POP Drop point, 3½" blade, stainless hilt and pins, wood Micarta scales $145

POP Drop point, 3½" blade, stainless steel hilt and pins, ivory Micarta scales, this man's work is really good $185

POP Drop point hunter, 3⅛" blade, nickel-silver hilt, ivory Micarta handle $155

PORTER Model A-1, 4½" cutting edge, blade, bolsters and butt all one piece, ivory Micarta handles $185

PRESS BUTTON KNIFE CO. Spearpoint, 4⅞" closed, nickel-silver bolsters, iron liners, jigged bone scales, if ever sharpened, it was not more than once, blade fully colored by time $375

PROUTY Fighter, 5¾" blade, brass hilt, butt and trim on sheath, walnut handle with fine figure ... $125

PROVIDENCE CUTLERY CO. Two-blade congress, 2½" closed, very fancy bolsters, nickel-silver liners and inlay nickel-silver and mother of pearl scales, an elegant little 100-year-old knife you can afford to carry, only lightly used $55

PUEDO Butterfly, 4¾" closed, damascus dagger blade, nickel-silver pins, damascus handle, black leather belt sheath $150

PUEDO Lockback push dagger, 3¾" damascus blade, stainless bolster and liners, gray iced celluloid scales, no sheath $125

PUEDO Lockback, 4⅜" closed, damascus bolster and blade, brass pins, stainless liners, wood slabs $100

PUEDO Mini-skinner, 2¼" damascus blade and tang, nickel-silver hilt, wood scales, no sheath, new $115

PUEDO Slipjoint, 4¼" closed, damascus frames, plastic pearl scales, considering this is the maker's second knife it is remarkable $100

PUGH Drop point skinner, 4¼" satin-finish filework blade and tang, wood slab handle $135

PUGH Survival, 10" satin-finish blade, wood scales $100

PULLIAM 5½" blade, osage orange handles $65

PULLIAM Camp, 8¾" blade, brass hilt, red curly maple handle, new $225

PUMA 4" blade, brass hilt, stag scales $75

PUMA 8½" blade, nickel-silver hilt and butt, stag scales, sheath, belt loop loose, from Super Set $100

PUMA Two-blade lockback, 4⅞" closed, clip and skinner blades, brass frame, jacaranda scales, box, new $125

PUMA Bootknife, 4½" clip point blade, integral hilt and butt stag inlays $125

PUMA Multi-blade horseman, 4¼" closed, brass liners nickel-silver bolsters, stag scales $220

PUMA Hunter, 4½" gutting blade, saw and corkscrew in handle, .800 silver inlay, stag scales $195

PUMA Sea Hunter, 6⅜" blade, aluminum hilt, red rubber handle, new $75

PUMA Sea Hunter, 6½" etched blade, steel hilt, red rubber handle $65

PUMA White Hunter, 6" blade, stainless hilt, brass pins, matched stag handle, lightly rusted blade edge $85

PUMA White hunter, 6" blade, aluminum hilt, India stag handle $95

PUMA White Hunter, 6" satin-finish blade, stainless hilt, brass pins, stag scales, original box, new $125

PUMA Lockback, 4″ closed, nickel-silver bolsters, brass liners black and white Micarta handle, new $75

PUMA Lockback, 4″ closed, nickel-silver bolsters, brass liners and inlay, wood Micarta scales, new $85

PUMA Lockback, 4″ closed, brass bolsters, liners and inlay, yellow Micarta scales, scrimmed Spirit of Massachusetts/Ship on reverse by LEV, #715, original box, new $125

PUMA Lockback, 4¼″ closed, gutting blade, bone saw, bird hook, corkscrew, nickel-silver bolsters, brass liners, stag scales, .800 silver inlay, new, box $175

PUMA Lockback, 4¼″ closed, threaded nickel-silver bolster, brass liners, stag scales, sharpened $85

PUMA Lockback, 4⅞″ closed, blade and bone saw, brass frames engraved by Lance Kelley, jacaranda scales $145

PUMA Lockback, 4⅞″ closed, blade and bone saw, brass frames jacaranda scales, leather pouch $105

PUMA Eddie Bauer lockback, 4″ closed, mirror finish blade, brass bolsters and liners, ivory Micarta slabs, belt sheath, new $85

PUMA Emperor lockback, 5½″ closed, brass frames, stag handle $125

PUMA Game Warden lockback, 4¾″ closed, brass frames, rosewood scales $95

PUMA Game Warden, 4⅞″ closed, lockback with gutting blade brass frames, jacaranda wood scales, box $95

PUMA Game Warden two-blade lockback, 5″ closed, brass bolsters liners and pins, wood scales $85

PUMA Game-Warden, 5″ closed, brass bolsters, pins, and liners, wood slabs, original box, new $75

PUMA Model 16-260 lockback, 3¾″ closed, white metal frames, black checkered inserts, leather pouch, box, new $40

PUMA Model 260, 3¾″ lockback, stainless frames, black checkered plastic scales $50

PUMA Model 715 four stars lockback, 4″ closed, brass liners, bolsters inlay and pins, ivory Micarta slabs, lighter in oval on slab-top, carried $75

PUMA Model 745 Lockback folding hunter, 4″ closed, brass bolsters and liners, India stag scales $115

PUMA Model 941 lockback, 4¼" closed, nickel-silver bolsters, brass liners, stag slabs, etched blade, used $75

PUMA Model 960 CUB lockback, 3⅞" closed, engraved bolsters, wood scales, carried, never sharpened $45

PUMA Model 970 Game Warden lockback, 5" closed, etched satin-finish single blade, brass bolsters, deer/moose inlays, ivory Micarta slabs scrimmed around inlays $145

PUMA Set of two Model 3588, large knife 8" blade, skinner 4" blade, nickel-silver hilts and butts, stag handles, wood chest for large knife, sheath for both $295

PUMA Model 3599, 9¾" blade, nickel-silver hilt and butt, .800 silver inlay, stag handle; wood box, new $225

PUMA Model 6377 White Hunter, 6" blade, aluminum hilt, brass pins stag slabs, no sheath, new $70

PUMA Model 6383 Buddy, 5" finn blade, nickel-silver hilt and butt, new, box, 15 year old quality $125

PUMA Original Bowie 6396, 6½" blade, aluminum hilt brass pins, stag slabs $65

PUMA Two-knife Super Set, 8⅝" Waioblatt and 4" Kleiner Jagdnicker, satin-finish blades, nickel-silver butts and hilts, stag scales, sheath, wood presentation box, new $420

PUMA Set of three lockbacks, 2⅞" closed, one stag, one jacaranda, one all stainless, engraved nickel-silver bolsters, wood and brass liners, all serial numbered #4, wooden presentation box $125

PUMA African Big Five Set, five knives, scrimmed brass frames, ivory Micarta scales, wood chest $345

PUMA Slipjoint Scale Knife, 6" closed, all stainless, checked handle, etched blade, original box, new $75

PUMA (GERMANY) Diver, 6½" blade, stainless hilt, red rubber handle, box, new $100

PUMA (GERMANY) Fisherman's, 6" closed, stainless blade with scaler, checkered steel handle, used $65

PUMA (GERMANY) Multi-blade horseman, 4⅜" closed, nickel-silver bolsters, brass liners, stag scales $175

PUMA (GERMANY) Lockback, 4″ closed, nickel-silver bolsters, brass liners, wood Micarta scales $65

PUMA (GERMANY) Puma Prince 911 lockback, 4¾″ closed, one blade and saw, blade etched 911 PUMA PRINCE, brass frames, stag scales, leather sheath, original box $150

PUMA (GERMANY) Model 35 Junior two-blade Wharncliffe, 3¾″ closed, nickel-silver bolsters, brass liners and inlay, exotic wood scales $45

PUMA (GERMANY) Model 1769 Commemorative lockback, 4¾″ closed, etched blade, engraved bolsters, brass frame, stag scales, serial #282, file work on spine, original wood display box $295

PUMA (SOLINGEN) Horseman, 4¼″ closed, nickel-silver bolsters, brass liners, stag slabs, used $135

PUMA-WERK 4¼″ blade, brass liners, corkscrew, hook and saw blades, stag handle $175

PURSLEY, AARON Skinner and caper set, 3″ blades, engraved ivory scales, no sheaths, a really nice pair, perfect ivory $465

PVM Butterfly, 5½″ closed, spear point blade, all stainless steel, no sheath $60

Q

QUEEN 4″ blade, aluminum butt, brass hilt, plastic stag handle $25

QUEEN Three-blade stock, 3⅝″ closed, nickel-silver bolsters, brass liners and pins, jigged bone scales $45

QUEEN Bicentennial Daddy Barlow, 5″ closed, nickel-silver bolsters, brass liners, black Micarta scales, serial #385 .... $20

QUEEN Bicentennial Daddy Barlow, 5″ closed, nickel-silver bolsters and inlay, brass liners, black delrin handle $45

QUEEN Letter opener, 5½″ blade, nickel-silver bolsters, brass liners pen knife in handle, bone scales, no sheath, very unusual $60

QUEEN Two-knife set: Straight, 4⅜″ blade, aluminum hilt and butt; folder, 3¾″ closed, nickel-silver bolsters and caps, brass liners, second cut stag scales $75

QUEEN CUTLERY Master Cutter Collection four-blade congress, 4″ closed, nickel-silver bolsters and inlay, brass liners, rosewood scales, serial #046, display box $50

QUEEN CUTLERY Three-carver Set, aluminum hilt and butt, stag inlays, stainless blades, new, no sheath $75

R

R.J.R. SHOE CO. Two-blade pen, 3⅛″ closed, nickel-silver scales, Star Brand Shoes Are Better on handle $45

RADOS Skinner, 4½″ Turkish damascus blade, nickel-silver hilt and butt, India stag handle, very distinctive damascus pattern $380

RANDALL 3¼″ blade, nickel-silver hilt, dural butt, stag handle, used, owner's name on blade back $145

RANDALL Astro model, 5¾″ blade, stainless hilt, black Micarta slab handle, sheath stone missing, new $235

RANDALL Bootknife, 3⅝″ satin-finish blade, brass pins and thong hole, ivory Micarta scales, new $255

RANDALL Bowie 1948-1952, 6″ blade, brass hilt, stag handle, mint, no sheath, not in current catalog $385

RANDALL Bootknife, 4″ blade, nickel-silver hilt, white, red and black spacers, burgundy Micarta handle, new $235

RANDALL Raymond Thorpe bowie, 13″ blade, nickel-silver hilt, alloy butt, rosewood handle, fine $365

RANDALL Clip point, 5½″ satin-finish blade, brass hilt, black finger-groove Micarta slabs, new $225

RANDALL Diver, 6¾″ stainless blade, brass hilt, black Micarta handle, diver's sheath with rubber leg straps and retainer ring, sharpened but not used) $225

RANDALL Fighter, 6″ x 1⅜″ high carbon steel blade, nickel-silver hilt, dural butt, leather handle, spacers show this is very old, sheath marked Model LS, one Randall I have not seen before $275

RANDALL Fighter, 6" blade, brass hilt, black Micarta handle, new $265

RANDALL Fighter, 6¾" blade, brass hilt, black Micarta finger-groove handle, owner's name etched on blade back $185

RANDALL Fighter, 7" blade, brass hilt, black Micarta handle $245

RANDALL Custom Model Vietnam Fighter, 6" blade, brass hilt, black Micarta handle, black coating (chipping off), 2 sheaths (carried, never used) $275

RANDALL Model 1 1950s, 7" blade, brass hilt, stag handle, no sheath, mint condition, made about 1948-1955 .... $435

RANDALL Model 1, 6" blade, brass hilt, red, white and black spacers, black Micarta handle ... $255

RANDALL Model 1, 6" clip point blade, brass hilt, black Micarta handle $265

RANDALL Model 1, 7" blade, brass hilt, red, white and black spacers, stag handle, ... $295

RANDALL Model 1, 7" satin-finish stainless blade, nickel-silver hilt, dural butt, black Micarta handle $265

RANDALL Model 1 Fighter, 6" blade, brass hilt, black Micarta handle, new $255

RANDALL Model 1 Fighter, 6⅛" blade, brass hilt, dural butt cap, leather handle, new $255

RANDALL Model 1 Fighter, 7" blade, brass hilt, dural butt, leather handle, new $225

RANDALL Model 1, 7" high carbon steel blade, brass hilt, dural butt, leather handle, old Randall, never used $245

RANDALL Model 1, 7" stainless blade, nickel-silver hilt, dural butt, black Micarta handle, black sheath $245

RANDALL Model 1, 7" stainless blade, nickel-silver hilt, dural butt, single finger-groove black Micarta handle $255

RANDALL Model 1, 7" blade, brass hilt, leather handle, Heiser sheath, a WW II Randall, used ... $775

RANDALL Model 1, 7" sawtooth-back blade, single brass hilt, leather handle, Vietnam-era, used there $385

RANDALL Model 1 Fighter, 8" blade, stag handle $245

RANDALL Model 1 Fighter, 8" blade, brass hilt, dural butt, leather handle, new $235

RANDALL Model 1 Bear Bowie, 8⅛" blade, brass hilt and butt, stag handle, new $345

RANDALL Model 2, 7" blade, brass hilt, stag handle, 40 years old, mint $1195

RANDALL Model 2 bootknife, 4" stainless blade, nickel-silver hilt, ivory Micarta scales, pocket or waistband sheath $235

RANDALL Model 2, 5" dagger blade, brass hilt, dural butt, leather handle $225

RANDALL Model 2, 7" dagger blade, brass hilt, dural butt, leather handle, 10-20 years old $275

RANDALL Model 2, 7" dagger blade, nickel-silver hilt, black Micarta handle, new $285

RANDALL Model 2, 8" dagger blade, brass hilt, dural butt, leather handle, new $235

RANDALL Model 2, 8" dagger blade, brass hilt, alloy butt cap, leather handle $245

RANDALL Model 2 Fighter, 6⅞" stainless dagger blade, nickel-silver hilt, alloy butt cap, black Micarta handle $275

RANDALL Model 2, 5" dagger blade, brass hilt, dural butt, leather handle $225

RANDALL Model 3, 6" stainless steel blade, nickel-silver hilt, India stag handle $205

RANDALL Model 3, 6" blade, nickel-silver hilt, finger-groove stag handle, no sheath, made about 1948, mint $365

RANDALL Model 3, 6" blade, brass hilt, aluminum butt, leather handle, 40 years old, shows age $475

RANDALL Model 3, 6" blade, brass hilt, finger-groove stag handle, 40 years old, blade shows age $595

RANDALL Model 3, 7" blade, brass hilt, stag handle, lightly used $165

RANDALL Model 3, 7" blade, brass hilt, stag handle, 40 years old, mint, H.H. Heiser sheath $695

RANDALL Model 4 clip point fighter, 5½" blade, brass hilt, black Micarta handle $235

RANDALL Model 4 hunter, 7" blade, brass-reinforced stacked hilt, India stag handle, trademark on stone-pouch cover, old, never used $575

RANDALL Model 5, 5" high carbon steel blade, brass hilt, dural butt, leather handle, used, excellent $165

RANDALL Model 5 camp and trail, 6" blade, brass hilt, dural butt, leather handle, sharpened .. $175

RANDALL Model 7, 7" high carbon steel blade, brass hilt, dural butt, leather handle, never used, never carried $195

RANDALL Model 8, 4" blade, brass hilt, stag handle, used $165

RANDALL Model 8, 4" blade, nickel-silver hilt, stag handle, red and gray spacers, used $165

RANDALL Model 8 Bird & Trout, 4" blade, brass hilt, stag handle, never carried or sharpened but probably used in kitchen or to cut fruit $215

RANDALL Model 8 Bird and Trout, 4" blade, brass hilt, stag handle, new $225

RANDALL Model 9 Pro Thrower, 10" overall, one-piece steel from ¼" stock, no sheath $75

RANDALL Model 10, 3" blade, brass pins and thong hole, rosewood slabs, two sheaths—belt w/snap and pocket, smallest Randall I've seen $115

RANDALL Custom Model 10 bootknife, 5" double-ground blade, rosewood handles, very nice indeed $135

RANDALL Model 10 kitchen, 7" blade, alloy handles $125

RANDALL Model 11 1950s, 5" blade, brass hilt, aluminum butt, leather handle, used, blade stained $185

RANDALL Model 19 1950s, Bushmaster, 4½" blade of ¼" stock, brass hilt, finger-groove stag handle, unused, sheath stone missing $275

RANDALL Model 11, 4½" blade, brass hilt, aluminum butt, red, black and white spacers, leather handle, new $175

RANDALL Model 11, 4½" blade, brass hilt, red, white and blue spacers, stag handle $195

RANDALL Model 11 Alaskan Skinner, 4" blade of ⅛"-stock, brass hilt, aluminum butt, leather handle, unused $195

RANDALL Model 11 Alaskan Skinner, 4" blade, brass hilt, stag handle, new $235

RANDALL Model 12, 9" blade, brass hilt and butt, red and black spacers, rosewood handle, sheath stone missing $495

RANDALL Model 12 bowie, 11" high carbon steel blade, brass-lugged hilt and butt, presentation grade walnut handle $495

RANDALL Model 12 Bear Bowie, 8" blade, brass hilt and butt cap, finger-grooved stag handle ... $345

RANDALL Model 12 Little Bear Bowie, 6" blade, brass hilt, dural butt, leather handle, used, never sharpened $225

RANDALL Model 12 Little Bear Bowie, 6" blade, nickel-silver hilt, dural butt, walnut handle, new $255

RANDALL Model 12 Little Bear Bowie, 6" high carbon steel blade, nickel-silver hilt, ivory Micarta handle $295

RANDALL Model 13 Arkansas toothpick, 6" dagger blade, fancy brass hilt and butt, white delrin handle, ... $495

RANDALL Model 14, 7½" stainless blade, brass hilt, black Micarta handle $265

RANDALL Model 14, 7½" blade, brass hilt, black Micarta finger-groove stag handle, new $245

RANDALL Model 14, 7½" stainless blade, brass hilt, black Micarta scales, brand new $245

RANDALL Model 14 Attack-Survival, 5½" high-carbon stainless steel blade, brass hilt, black Micarta handle, new $255

RANDALL Model 14 Bowie, 7½" blade, brass hilt, black Micarta finger-groove stag handle, not used, shows age $225

RANDALL Model 14 clip point, 7½" blade, nickel-silver hilt, aluminum butt, stag handle, red black and white spacers, new $295

RANDALL Model 14 Fighter, 7½" clip point blade, brass hilt, finger groove black Micarta handle, customer's name on blade $245

RANDALL Model 18 Attack-Survival, 7½" sawtooth-back blade, brass hilt and butt cap, stainless hollow handle, new $255

RANDALL Model 19, 4½" blade, brass hilt, stag handle, 10-20 years old $245

RANDALL Model 20, 4½" blade, brass hilt, red, white and black spacers, stag handle $195

RANDALL Model 21 1950s, 3¼" blade, brass hilt, red, black and white spacers, stag handle .. $185

RANDALL Model 21, 3¼" blade, brass hilt, red, black and white spacers, stag handle $185

RANDALL Model 21, 3⅜" skinner blade, brass hilt, stag handle $175

RANDALL Model 21, 3⅜" blade, brass hilt, stag handle, new $225

RANDALL Model 23, 4½" high carbon steel blade, brass hilt, black Micarta scales $195

RANDALL Model 23, 4½" blade, brass hilt, stag handle, new $215

RANDALL Model 25, 6" blade, dural hilt and butt, leather and stag handle, new $255

RANDALL Smithsonian Bowie, 10¾" blade, brass hilt, dural butt, leather handle, 10-20 years old $455

RANDALL Smithsonian bowie, 11" overall, brass-lugged hilt, stag handle, trademark on snaps, old $695

RANDALL Sportsman bowie, 8¾" stainless blade, curved hilt, India stag handle $395

RANDALL Sportsman bowie, 9" blade, brass-lugged hilt and butt, walnut handle $385

RANDALL Stiletto, 5⅞" blade, fancy brass hilt and butt, ivory Micarta handle $285

RANDALL Miniature survival, 3½" blade, brass hilt and butt, stainless hollow handle, only 100 made $985

RANDALL Survival, 7⅜" spear point blade, brass hilt and butt cap, all steel hollow handle $295

RANDALL Survival, 7⅜" spear point blade, sawtooth back, brass hilt and brass cap, all steel hollow handle, small nick in hilt $285

RANDALL Survival, 7½" sawtooth-back blade, brass hilt, steel hollow handle, early knife, not used, light rust on handle $295

RANDALL Survival, 5½" sawtooth 440C blade, brass hilt and O-ring-sealed screw cap, stainless steel tube handle, early version second handle model $285

RANDALL (SOLINGEN) Fighter, 7¼" blade, brass hilt, wood handle, new $155

REE Drop point, 2⅝" blade, engraved nickel-silver bolsters, snakewood scales $65

REE Drop point, 3" blade, brass engraved hilt, wood scales, new $65

REEVE, CHRIS 8¾" blade, one piece tool steel, strongest hollow handle design $235

REEVE, CHRIS One-piece Airman with saw, 4" blade, #57, used $135

REEVE, CHRIS Clip point, 4" one-piece steel blade, hollow handle, very nice, sharpened, not used $115

REEVE, CHRIS One-piece clip point, 4" blade, aluminum butt cap, hollow handle $125

REEVE, CHRIS Tanto #1, 7" blade, entire knife machined from one piece of tool steel $225

REMINGTON 4⅛" blade, steel hilt and butt, black plastic handle, used, blade pitted, no sheath $45

REMINGTON Boy Scout, 3¾" closed, nickel-silver bolster, ring and shield, brass liners, jigged bone scales, used $65

REMINGTON Butcher, 9" blade, wood handle, well used, no sheath $20

REMINGTON Model R1263 two-blade jack, 5⅜" closed, satin-finish etched blade, nickel-silver bolsters and bullet inlay, brass liners, delrin jigged bone scales $150

REMINGTON Model R1613 toothpick, 5" closed, etched satin-finish blade, R1613 blade back, nickel-silver bolsters and bullet inlay, brass liners, jigged bone delrin scales, ... $75

REMINGTON Model R1615 toothpick, 5" closed, satin-finish blade, nickel-silver bolsters, brass liners, red, yellow and white striped celluloid scales $75

REMINGTON Model #R4353 1985 two-blade, 4⅛" closed, nickel-silver bolsters and cartridge inlay, brass liners, jigged bone scales $75

REMINGTON Muskrat, 3⅝" spay and California clip blades, nickel-silver bolsters, brass liners, sterling bullet inlay, delrin bone scales, serial #3400/5000, new, box $95

REMINGTON Peanut, 2¾" closed, brass liners, nickel-silver bolsters, delrin scales $30

REMINGTON Skinner, 6¼" blade, wood handle, well used, no sheath $20

REMINGTON Fisherman single-blade slipjoint, 5" closed, satin-finish blade etched REMINGTON, nickel-silver bolsters and inlay, brass liners, red and yellow plastic scales, new, original box $35

REMINGTON Texas toothpick, 1987, 5" closed, nickel-silver bolsters, caps and cartridge inlay, bone delrin scales, box $75

REMINGTON (GERMANY) Three—blade counterfeit sleeveboard whittler, 3½" closed, nickel-silver bolsters, brass liners, fine pearl scales, c. 1972 .... $135

REMINGTON UMC (SOLINGEN) Two-blade swell center jack, 5" closed nickel-silver bolsters and inlay, brass liners and pins, jigged bone scales, used, blade reground $35

RICKE Drop point hunter, 3⅞" blade, tapered tang, nickel-silver hilt, black and brown Micarta scales $75

RICKE Drop point hunter, 4¾" blade, tapered tang, nickel-silver hilt, ivory Micarta scales $125

RICKE Lockback, 3⅜" closed, nickel-silver bolsters and liners, nicely matched stag slabs, carried $125

RIGID Three-blade stock, 3⅜" closed, satin-finish blade, nickel-silver bolsters, brass liners, wood scales, new, original box $45

RIGID Bootknife, 3¼" blade, black linen Micarta scales $75

RIGID Bootknife, 3¾" blade, stainless hilt and butt, ivory Micarta handle $55

RIGID Drop point 3⅜" satin-finish blade, stainless hilt and pins, wood slabs, new, original box $50

RIGID Bootknife, 3¾" satin-finish blade, nickel-silver pins, black Micarta slabs, very slim $75

RIGID Lockback, 3⅜" closed, stainless bolsters and liners, yellow Micarta scales, original box ... $35

RIGID Lockback, 5⅛" closed, brass bolsters, liners and pins, wood finger-groove slabs, satin-finish blade, leather belt sheath $45

RIGID Lockback, 5⅛" closed, satin-finish up-sweptblade, brass bolsters, liners and pins, wood finger-groove slabs, leather sheath $55

RIGID Skinner, 3" blade, nickel-sliver hilt, wood slab handle, new, original box $30

RIGID SHAW-LIEBOWITZ Skinner, 4¼" blade etched Boston Tea Party, brass hilt and butt, rosewood handle, serial #20 .... $165

RIGID Skinner, 5⅜" blade, brass hilt (small nick) and butt, rosewood scales, unused $75

RIMPLER Guthook, 3" well-ground blade, wood Micarta scales, guthook point should be blunted for proper action $65

ROATH Caper, 2⅜" blade, burgundy Micarta scales $45

ROBERTSON, J.D. Fighter, 6¾" blade, brass hilt and butt, exotic wood handle $125

ROBESON Shuredge clip point, 4" closed, aluminum hilt and butt, leather handle, sharpened and used $30

ROBESON Shuredge Daddy Barlow, 5" closed, nickel-silver bolsters, brass liners, red bone scales, used, polished $65

ROBESON CUTLERY Swell center pen, 3" closed, nickel-silver bolsters, brass liners, nice pearl scales, blades pitted $45

ROCHFORD Bowie, 10¼" blade, tapered tang, curly maple handle with finger grooves, new $305

RODGERS, JOSEPH Four-blade congress, 3¼" closed, nickel-silver rat tail bolsters, brass liners, mother of pearl scales, suede purse, may not have been used but about 100 years old $145

RODGERS, JOSEPH (SHEFFIELD) Bowie, 7¾" spearpoint blade badly pitted near point, nickel-silver hilt inlay, stag scales, no sheath $175

RODGERS, JOSEPH (ENGLAND) Four-blade congress, 3½" closed, nickel-silver bolsters and inlay, stag scales $85

RODGERS-WOSTENHOLM (ENGLAND) NKCA 1978 three-blade canoe, 3⅝" closed, nickel-silver bolsters, brass liners, jigged bone scales $65

ROGER-WOSTENHOLM Three-blade NKCA canoe, 3¾" closed, nickel-silver bolsters and inlay, brass liners, jigged bone scales, serial #2097 ...... $60

RODGERS, WILLIAM clip point hunter, 4½" blade, brass hilt and spacers, alloy butt, leather handle, pre-WW II, poor finish but very usable $35

RODGERS, WILLIAM I Cut My Way trademarked two-blade even-end pen, 3¼" closed, nickel-silver inlay, brass liners, buffalo horn scales, two small chips on one side, 80-100 years old $60

RODGERS, WILLIAM Two-blade sleeveboard pen, 3¼" closed, brass liners, nickel-silver inlay, shadow pattern tortoise shell or celluloid scales, original poor tip on main blade, unused though 40-70 years old $45

RODGERS, WILLIAM (ENGLAND) Two-blade gentleman's pocket sleeveboard, 3¾" closed, nickel-silver bolsters and liners, very nice ivory scales with one small check, very fine condition, old, unusual feature—spring tapered at each end $125

RODGERS, WILLIAM Two-blade sleeveboard pen, 3¾" closed, brass liners, nickel-silver bolsters and inlay, ivory scales $125

RICHARD, RON Button lock, 4¼" closed, stainless steel blade and bolsters, ivory scales $535

RUANA 5" blade, aluminum frame, stag inlay handle $115

RUANA 5" scratched blade, aluminum frame, stag inlay handle $175

RUANA 6¼" blade, aluminum frame, stag inlay handle, old $175

RUANA 9⅜" blade, brass hilt and butt, stag handle $225

RUANA Bowie, 7" brass-backed blade, brass hilt, stag slabs, used $255

RUANA Bowie, 9" blade, brass hilt and butt, India stag scales, new $275

RUANA Bowie, 9⅜" blade, brass hilt and butt, elk horn scales, belt-stud sheath, new $255

RUANA Bowie, 9⅞" blade, brass hilt and pins, stag slabs, made by Rudy $345

RUANA Camp, 7¾" brass-backed blade, brass butt and hilt, India stag scales, new $195

RUANA Camp, 9" blade, aluminum frame, stag inlay, old $240

RUANA Camp, 9" blade, aluminum frame, stag inlay, old $255

RUANA Camp, 9" blade, aluminum, elk horn handle, the only one I have seen $345

RUANA Camp, 9⅛" blade, alloy handle, elk horn inserts, new custom model $135

RUANA Clip point hunter, 6" blade, aluminum frame and pins, stag inlays, used, made before Rudy's death $135

RUANA Finn, 4" blade, aluminum, elk horn handle, new $95

RUANA Fighter, 6½" brass-backed blade, aluminum, elk horn, used, excellent $185

RUANA Fighter, 7" blade, brass hilt, stag slabs used, not old $185

RUANA Fighter, 7¼" blade, aluminum, elk horn, new $155

RUANA Fighter, 7½" blade, aluminum frame, bone inlay handle, used $150

RUANA Hunter, 4" blade, aluminum hilt and butt, elk horn inlays, older knife $235

RUANA Hunter, 5" blade, aluminum hilt and butt, elk horn inlays, older knife $245

RUANA Hunter, 6" blade, aluminum, elk horn handle, used, very good $225

RUANA Hunter, 6" bowie blade, aluminum frame, stag inlay handle $100

RUANA Hunter, 7" blade, aluminum elk horn, used, excellent $215

RUANA Model 29A Fighter, 6½" brass-backed blade, aluminum hilt and butt, stag scales, signed by Rudy in 1976 .... $235

RUANA Model 30AM Bowie, 10" brass-backed blade, aluminum hilt and butt, stag inlays .. $325

RUANA Model 31BBM Bowie, 7½" blade, brass hilt and pins, elk horn scales $300

RUANA Model 32BM Davey Crockett Bowie, 9¼"
blade, brass hilt, aluminum butt, half horse, half alli-
gator walnut handle $295

RUANA Model 35BM Bowie, 9⅛" brass-backed
blade dated 1977, aluminum, elk horn inlays $325

RUANA Model 38C Bowie, 12¼" blade, brass hilt,
butt and blade back inlay, made before Rudy
retired $455

RUANA Model 38C Bowie, 8" blade, brass hilt and
butt, elk horn scales, brass-back blade, new $220

RUANA Model 39C bowie, 9" brass-backed blade,
brass hilt and butt, elk horn scales $345

RUANA Model 40A Bowie, 9½" brass-backed ⅜"-
thick blade, brass hilt and butt, India stag
handle $295

RUANA Model 40D, 7½" blade, brass hilt and butt
cap, wood handle, used, old, rough $175

RUANA Model 42DM Bowie, 9⅝" spearpoint blade,
brass hilt and butt, elk horn handle $325

RUANA Skinner, 5" blade, very unusual brass hilt
and butt, finger grooved stag handle marked
1978 .... $295

RUANA Skinner, 6" blade, aluminum frame, stag
inlay handle, new $140

RUANA Skinner, 6⅛" blade, aluminum frame, stag
inlays, used $265

RUANA Sticker, 7¼" blade, alloy handle, elk horn
inlays, new custom model $125

RUANA Survival, 6" blade, cord-wrapped handle,
used $75

RUANA Tanto, 7¼" blade, brass bolsters, ebony
handle, new $165

RUSSELL, A.G. 110 IR lockback, 3¼" closed,
stainless bolsters, inlay and liners, ivory Rucarta
slabs $30

RUSSELL, A.G. FH-2 split bolsterlock, 4" closed,
stainless bolsters, liners, pins and cap, jigged bone
scales, #1549 of 1600, unused, original box .. $70

RUSSELL, A.G. Bowie, 12" brass-backed blade,
brass hilt and butt, India stag scales, only 35
made $495

RUSSELL, A.G. Gent's hunter, 2¾" blade, nickel-
silver hilt, brass pins, ivory Rucarta slabs ... $125

RUSSELL, A.G. Lockback, 3⅝" closed, alloy
frames, coral Rucarta scales, handmade, no longer
made $195

RUSSELL, A.G. Lockback, 5⅛" closed, alloy frames,
black Micarta scales, only six made this size $185

RUSSELL, A.G. 1977 Sting bootknife, 3¼" blade, red liners, stainless hilt, butt and pins, stag slabs, very early Sting, marked Springdale, Ark. $155

RUSSELL, A.G. Sting IAT bootknife, 3¼" high-carbon stainless non-reflective black blade, new $45

RUSSELL, A.G. Sting II bootknife, 3¾" blade, integral hilt and butt, black linen Micarta scales, hard to get $75

RUSSELL, A.G. Sting II, 3¾" blade, integral hilt and butt, rosewood scales $85

RUSSELL, A.G. Elmer Keith-Harvey Draper tribute, 6⅜" ⅜"-thick stainless steel blade, nickel-silver hilt and butt, fileworked brass collar, stag handle $495

RUSSELL, A.G. (GERMANY) Safety axe, used $65

RUSSELL, A.G./CAMILLUS CM-2 Grandaddy Barlow, 5" closed, nickel-silver bolsters and inlay, brass liners, jigged bone scales, #1887, new $60

RUSSELL, A.G./CATTARAUGUS CM-10 20th Century Barlow, 3¼" closed, nickel-silver bolsters and inlay, brass liners, jigged bone scales, #315, new, original box $45

RUSSELL, A.G./CATTARAUGUS CM-11 lockback, 2⅝" closed, stainless bolsters, inlay and liners, jigged bone scales, #1318, new, original box $30

RUSSELL, A.G./CATTARAUGUS CM-12, split bolsterlock, 3" closed, stainless bolsters, liners and inlay, jigged bone scales, #1318, new, original box $35

RUSSELL, A.G./CATTARAUGUS FH-1 split bolsterlock, 4⅝" closed, nickel-silver bolsters, liners and inlay, jigged bone scales, #1270, new, original box $45

RUSSELL, A.G./CATTARAUGUS Liberty two-blade shadow pattern, 3½" closed, engraved Statue of Liberty brass scales, #1355, new, original box ... $20

RUSSELL, A.G./HEN & ROOSTER Two-blade sleeveboard lobster, 2¾" closed, engraved stainless scales, mint condition $225

RUSSELL, A.G./HEN & ROOSTER 1976 coffin-handle slipjoint, 3⅝" closed, deeply embossed American eagle on one side, shield and banner on other, all stainless steel $135

RUSSELL, A.G./HEN & ROOSTER 1976 Bicentennial coffin-handle slipjoint, 3¾ closed, sterling silver handles, embossed eagle/banner and shield $220

RUSSELL, A.G./HEN & ROOSTER 1976 Entebbe single blade and screwdriver/cap-lift, 2⅞" closed, sterling silver handle, mint, original box, commemorates Entebbe airport rescue July 4th, 1976, 100 made in silver, 400 in stainless $230

RUSSELL, A.G./HEN & ROOSTER CM-4 slipjoint baby barlow, 2 ½" closed, nickel-silver bolsters and liners, ivory scales, serial #1529 .... $135

RUSSELL, A.G./HEN & ROOSTER KCC CM-5 Model three-blade whittler, 3⅝" closed, nickel-silver bolsters, inlay and liners, African blackwood handle, rarest CM, Serial #1111 of 1200 .... $160

RUSSELL, A.G./PUMA CM-3 Wharncliffe jack, 3¾" closed, nickel-silver bolsters, caps and Luger pistol inlay, brass liners $95

RUSSELL, A.G./SCHRADE CUTLERY CM-1 three-blade stock, 4" closed, blade etched The Kentucky Rifle, nickel-silver bolster and inlay, brass liners, ivory delrin scales, #13018, new $95

RUSSELL, D.H. (CANADA) Slim Canadian Belt, 4" stainless blade, rosewood handles $45

RUSSELL, J. & CO. (GREEN RIVER WORKS) Two-blade barlow, 3⅜" closed, blade etched 1875-1975 Commemorative Issue, #8008, nickel-silver engraved bolster, brass liners, orange delrin scales $60

RUSSELL, J. & CO. (GREEN RIVER WORKS) Limited edition, old Green River Barlow, serial #502, cedar box $85

RUSSELL, J. & CO. (GREEN RIVER WORKS) Skinner, 6" blade, wood handle, scratched, pitted but never used, no sheath $25

RUSSELL, J. & CO. (GREEN RIVER WORKS) Bicentennial Set of three in presentation box (1834-1976): Dadley, Buffalo Skinner and Hunter, satin-finish blades, serial #101, ebony handles with brass inlays $245

RUSSELL, J. & CO. (GREEN RIVER WORKS) Eight very old ivory-handled table knives $180

RUSSELL, J. & CO. (GREEN RIVER WORKS) Table knife, 5⅝" blade, no sheath, I think scales are hard rubber, little use, old $20

S

S & D BULLDOG BRAND Two-blade slipjoint canoe, 3½" closed, blade etched Our Best, nickel-silver bolsters, liners, and inlay, stag scales, new .. $50

S.W. CUTLERY Serpentine, 3¾" closed, nickel-silver bolsters, brass liners, Paul Revere Commemorative $20

S.W. CUTLERY Serpentine, 3¾" closed, nickel-silver bolsters, brass liners, Liberty Bell Commemorative $30

S.W. CUTLERY Serpentine, 3¾" closed, nickel-silver bolsters, brass liners, Minute Man Commemorative $25

S.W. CUTLERY Set of five commemorating Patrick Henry, John Adams, Nathan Hale, Thomas Jefferson and George Washington: all serpentine, 4" closed, nickel-silver bolsters, brass liners, all serial #1476 .... $105

SABRE Monarch 7¼" blade etched Original Bowie Knife, stainless butt and hilt, stag handle $30

SANDERS Bayonet, steel hilt and butt, wood handle $35

SANDERS, ATHERN 9" blade, brass hilt and butt cap, light stag handle, slight pitting $50

SASSER Fighter, 5" blade, stainless hilt and pins, stag handle and sheath $385

SAWBY, S.W. Buttonlock, 4¼" closed, stainless frames, filework, abalone inlays, absolutely beautiful $545

SAWBY, S.W. Buttonlock, 4" closed, hollow-ground blade, stainless bolsters, button and filework liners, burgundy Micarta slabs, #147, very slim $275

SAWBY Interframe lockback, 3⅞" closed, stainless frame, ironwood and abalone inlays, beautiful and unusual $455

SCHEPERS 3½" cable damascus blade and tang, brass hilt $55

SCHEPERS 3⅞" damascus blade, brass hilt, cattle horn handle $85

SCHEPERS 4" cable damascus blade, stag horn handle, buffalo nickel butt cap $75

SCHEPERS 4¼" damascus blade, fileworked damascus hilt, whale tooth handle with scrimshaw (legal, documents included) $650

SCHEPERS 5⅛" damascus blade, tapered tang, brass pins, ivory slabs, filework blade back, no sheath $185

SCHEPERS 7" damascus blade, brass hilt, very nice cattle horn handle, no sheath $195

SCHEPERS Dagger, 4½" damascus blade, hilt ferrule and pommel, mastodon ivory handle, no sheath $240

SCHEPERS Dagger, 5½" damascus blade, nickel-silver engraved hilt and butt cap, stag handle $175

SCHEPERS Dagger, 6¼" damascus blade, filework brass hilt, carved walnut handle, no sheath $225

SCHEPERS Drop point, 4½" damascus blade and hilt, buffalo horn handle, no sheath $185

SCHEPERS Drop point hunter, 5¼" damascus blade, fileworked integral bolster, ivory scales $355

SCHEPERS Kris, 7" damascus blade, filework hilt, and butt, amber and stag handle, red spacers $135

SCHEPERS Tomahawk, 3½" damascus blade, 14" hickory handle $135

SCHEPERS Tomahawk, 3¾" hand forged blade, 17" hickory handle $75

SCHLIEPER, CARL (Eye Brand) Texas toothpick, 5" closed, nickel-silver bolsters, caps and inlay, brass liners, stag scales $85

SCHMIDT & ZIGLER Three-blade stock, 3⅝" closed, nickel-silver bolsters and inlays, brass liners, ivory scales, blade etched Schmidt & Ziegler Stock Knife El Toro $75

SCHNEIDER Bowie, 9⅛" blade, stainless steel hilt, nickel-silver butt, ivory scales, BL catalog #573, his first bowie, unmarked, a fine demonstration of work to come, no sheath $3,495

SCHNEIDER Bowie, 9¼" blade, stainless hilt, stag scales, no sheath, BL catalog #572 .... $2,495

SCHNEIDER Caper, 3" hand-rubbed flat-ground 154CM blade, stainless steel bolsters, mother of pearl scales, no sheath $635

SCHNEIDER Dagger, 6" 154CM blade, stainless bolster, India stag scales no sheath $395

SCHNEIDER Dagger, 6⅜" blade, hand-rubbed finish, very tapered tang, McKenzie-engraved stainless bolsters and pins, perfectly matched stag scales $2,375

SCHNEIDER Drop point, 3½" 154CM blade, nickel-silver hilt forms whale's flukes, ivory handle artfully formed into a whale tooth, scrimmed by Metcalf, no sheath $685

SCHRADE Two-blade barlow, 3¾" closed, fancy nickel-silver bolsters, brass liners, ivory color scales with scrimmed ducks $30

SCHRADE Two-blade folding hunter, 5¼" closed, nickel-silver bolsters, brass liners, ivory delrin scales factory scrimmed, leather sheath, box $25

SCHRADE Clasp, 5½" closed, blade etched Custer's Last Stand, nickel-silver bolsters and caps, brass liners, India stag scales $125

SCHRADE Drop point, 3¾" 440A blade, brass bolster, improved brown delrin handle, after success of the Schrade-Loveless, Schrade made this copy without Loveless name to sell for less, serial #678 .... $115

SCHRADE Jack, 3⅝" closed, nickel-silver bolsters, brass liners, celluloid scales, safety award to DeQueen and Hatfield Mill Workers 1926, lightly sharpened $60

SCHRADE Cut C Jack, 4½" closed, steel bolsters and liners, wood scales, pre WW II $65

SCHRADE Old Timer (The) single-blade linerlock jack, 2 13/16" closed, brass liners, nickel-silver bolsters and inlay, plastic handles, original box, new $20

SCHRADE/COLT Bowie, 6½" blade etched by Aurum, brass hilt, butt cap and etched inlay, wood Micarta handle, wood display box, no sheath $225

SCHRADE/LOVELESS Drop point, 3½" 440A blade, gold and silver etched by Shaw-Liebowitz, Proof brass bolster, ivory delrin scrimmed whaling scene $365

SCHRADE/LOVELESS Drop point, 3⅝" 154CM blade, brass bolster, brown delrin handle, #3344 .... $165

SCHRADE/LOVELESS 3⅝" satin-finish blade, brass hilt and pins, tapered tang, red delrin handle, original box, #1179, new $225

SCHRADE/WALDEN Fruit, 5¾" closed, stainless serrated blade, etched Wonda-Edge, brass liners, ivory Micarta slabs $65

SCHRADE/WALDEN Sailor's, 4⅛" closed, satin-finish blade, nickel-silver bolsters, brass liners, jigged bone scales, unused $40

SCHRADE/WOSTENHOLM IXL Three-blade Wharncliffe stock, 4 ⅞" closed, nickel-silver bolsters and inlay, brass liners, rosewood scales, 1787-1980 limited edition $40

SCHROCK Bootknife, 3⅜" mirror-finish blade, tapered tang, brass pins and thong hole, red and black liners, wood scales with finger grooves, new $95

SCORPION (ENGLAND) Survival, 8⅛" sawtooth-back blade, fuller steel hilt, cord-wrapped hollow handle, very unusual $75

SEABOARD STEEL CO (FRANCE) Tool, 5½" closed, all stainless steel, used $150

SEARS, HENRY & SONS 1865 Serpentine lobster pen, 3" closed, nickel-silver tips, green celluloid scales, small chip from one, used $30

SEARS CRAFTSMAN Two-blade serpentine jack, 3¼" closed, brass liners, bolster and emblem, wood scales, 100th Anniversary $60

SEARS CRAFTSMAN Three-blade stock, 4" closed, brass liners and bolsters, laminated hardwood scales, original box, new $35

SEARS CRAFTSMAN Three-blade serpentine stock (Bowie Stock Knife), 4" closed, brass liners, nickel-silver bolsters, ivory delrin scales, original box, new $45

SEGUINE, L.W. Upswept hunter, 4½" blade, finger groove wood scales $155

SEGUINE, M.W. Fighter, 5½" blade, brass hilt and butt, moose horn finger-groove handle, used, fine condition, sheath not original $335

SEGUINE, M.W. Hunter, 5" blade, brass hilt and butt, exotic wood handle, sharpened, never used or carried $245

SEGUINE, M.W. Standard hunter, 5" blade, brass hilt and butt, mesquite handle, very rare ... $345

SEGUINE, M.W. Hunter, 5½" blade, brass hilt and butt, bone finger-groove handle, used, never sharpened, no sheath $245

SEGUINE, M.W. Skinner, 5" blade, brass hilt and butt, moose horn handle, Merle's deluxe version $425

SERVEN, JIM Buttonlock, 5½" closed, satin-finish blade, stainless interframe, skull crusher, wood and black Micarta inlays, new $445

SERVEN, JIM Interframe lockback, 2½" closed, stainless frame, pink ivory inlay handle $195

SERVEN, JIM Lockback bootknife, 4¼" closed, nickel-silver bolsters and liners, two-piece cattle horn scales, small crack at pin, #268, new .. $265

SERVEN, JIM Lockback Street Fighter, 5" closed, stiletto blade, stainless bolsters and liners, rosewood scales, filework back, #216 .... $225

SERVEN, JIM Lockback Street Fighter, 5" closed, stiletto blade, nickel-silver bolsters, caps and liners, turquoise scales, filework back #272 ...... $335

SERVEN, JIM Lockback, 4¼" closed, stainless blade and bolsters, Buffalo horn scales, stainless steel liners and bolsters, India stag scales, filework locking bar and blade-back, engraved, early work by fine maker $145

SERVEN, JIM Midlock, 5" closed, stainless bolsters, filework liners and blade, wood scales $195

SHAW-LIEBOWITZ & CASE Two-blade pen, 3⅛" closed, solid sterling silver and gold handles, bears on each side $295

SHAW-LIEBOWITZ & CASE Two-blade pen, Model 5275, SP, 3⅛" closed, solid sterling handles with Lake Placid Olympics, very rare $200

SHAW-LIEBOWITZ & CASE Folder, 4½" closed, etched with a moose, serial #50 .... $110

SHAW-LIEBOWITZ/SCHRADE Uncle Henry stock, 4" closed, etched with Raccoon, serial #50 .. $85

SHAW, DAVID Bootknife, 4¼" single-edge blade, very tapered tang, stainless pins, red liners, cocobolo scales, hand-rubbed finish, another outstanding maker $165

SHAW, DAVID 4⅜" flat ground hand-rubbed 154CM, nickel-silver hilt, rosewood handle $145

SHAW, DAVID Bowie, 7⅞" flat ground hand-rubbed blade, nickel-silver hilt and butt, rosewood scales, no sheath $535

SHAW, DAVID California bowie, 5" blade, nickel-silver scabbard and trim, rosewood handle $435

SHARP, J. Bowie, 7¾" blade, steel hilt, ironwood handle, Nice work for a maker I never heard of $225

SHIVA KI Bootknife, 3½" damascus blade, all steel $225

SHIVA KI Fighter, 9" blade, brass hilt, pins, exotic wood handle, designer's name stamped into back of blade $395

SIGMAN Bird and trout, 3" blade, very tapered tang, nickel-silver bolster, ivory scales, gorgeous hand-painted scrimshaw by Michael Collins $985

SIGMAN Bootknife, 4¼″ blade, stainless hilt, oosic scales, outstanding $445

SIGMAN Drop point, 3¾″ blade, etched buck in gold by Shaw-Liebowitz, nickel-silver hilt, pins and inlay, burgundy Micarta scales $345

SIGMAN Drop point, 4″ blade, nickel-silver bolsters, perfectly matched stag scales $365

SIGMAN Fighter, 6⅜″ blade, nickel-silver bolsters, oosic scales, right and left hand sheaths ... $595

SIGMAN Hunter, 3″ blade, nickel-silver bolster, sterling pins, ivory scales, cracked both sides $285

SIGMAN Clip point hunter, 5″ hollow-ground 154CM blade, nickel-silver hilt, black Micarta scales, left-hand sheath, small scratches, one side of point $325

SIGMAN Clip point hunter, 5¾″ blade, super-hollow-grind, nickel-silver hilt, black Micarta scales, left-hand sheath, great for the man who wants a big knife $355

SIGMAN Clip point hunter, 5⅞″ hollow-ground blade, nickel-silver hilt, black Micarta scales $395

SIGMAN Straight hunter, 4¾″ flat ground hand-rubbed blade, nickel-silver bolsters, sterling pins, ivory handles, cracked both sides $285

SIGMAN, C.R. 3⅞″ blade, very tapered tang, coral liners, nickel-silver hilt, ivory Micarta slab handle, deer scene/flowers scrimmed by SKM $355

SIGMAN, C.R. Fighter, 5″ mirror-polish blade, nickel-silver hilt, tapered tang, wood Micarta slab handle $395

SIGMAN, C.R. Hunter, 4″ satin-finish blade, brass hilt and pins, wood Micarta scales, no sheath, new $60

SIGMAN, C.R. Hunter, 4″ mirror-finish blade, very tapered tang, nickel-silver hilt, pins and inlay, ivory Micarta slabs, red liners $295

SIGMAN, C.R. Skinner, 4″ mirror-finish blade, brass hilt, aluminum butt, zebra wood finger-groove handle $285

SIGMAN, C.R. Clip point skinner, 4½″ mirror-finish blade, nickel-silver hilt, stag handle $295

SIGMAN, C.R. Nesmuk skinner, 4¼″ flat ground hand-rubbed blade, nickel-silver hilt, yellow Micarta scales $225

SIGMAN, CORBET 2¾″ hand-rubbed, flat ground blade, nickel-silver bolsters, sterling silver pins, ivory handles, some splitting $245

SIGMAN, CORBET 4¾" hand-rubbed flat ground 154CM blade, nickel-silver bolsters and inlay, sterling pins around handle, ivory scales, some splitting, part of the Blevins collection $295

SILVER DOLLAR (GERMANY) Two-blade jack, 5½" closed, etched blade, nickel-silver bolsters, brass liners, jigged bone scales $85

SILVER DOLLAR BRAND Two-blade trapper, 5¾" closed, nickel-silver bolsters, brass liners, plastic scales $50

SIMMONS (GERMANY) Four-blade congress, 3⅝" closed, nickel-silver bolsters and inlay, brass liners, stag scales, Bee on triangle stamp $85

SIMMONS HARDWARE CO (GERMANY) Three-blade stock, 4" closed, nickel-silver bolsters and inlay, brass liners, nicely matched stag slabs, #2397 on blade $175

SINYARD Fighter, 6" blade, stainless hilt and butt, stag handle $185

SITES Clip point, 5" blade, brass hilt and butt, stag handle $95

SITES Drop point, 4" blade, stainless hilt and pins, wood Micarta scales $90

SITES Drop point skeleton, 3¾" blade, filework around tang $75

SITES Skinner, 2½" blade, stainless hilt, stag handle $85

SKY, BOB Bowie, 10" mirror-finish blade, stainless hilt and butt, rosewood handle, new $635

SKY, BOB Chute, 4⅞" satin-finish clip point blade, tapered tang, nickel-silver hilt, black Micarta slabs, new $225

SKY, BOB Clip point, 3½" blade, tapered tang, nickel-silver hilt and pins, white iced celluloid scales $95

SKY, BOB Dagger, 12" blade, nickel-silver hilt and butt, ivory scales, a big Arkansas Toothpick $325

SKY KNIVES, BOB Bowie, 7¼" mirror-finish blade, stainless hilt and butt, stag slabs, no sheath, zipper case, new $295

SKY KNIVES, BOB Clip point fighter, 8½" mirror-polish blade, engraved nickel-silver hilt, sub-hilt and butt, ivory and burgundy Micarta slabs, new $495

SLAUGHTER 2¾" sawtooth-back blade, all stainless steel $45

SMALL 3¼" blade, brass bolsters, ivory Micarta handle $95

SMALL 3⅛" blade, nickel-silver bolster engraved by Howard Grant, ivory Micarta handle, used very little $160

SMALL, ED Hunter, 5" damascus steel blade, brass hilt and butt, curly maple handle, a working knife $255

SMALL, JIM Drop point, 4⅛" blade, nickel-silver hilt, African blackwood scales $155

SMALL, JIM Small hunter, 3" blade, engraved nickel-silver bolsters, walrus ivory scales ... $255

SMITH, CARY Clip point, 4" blade, brass hilt and butt, rosewood handle, early work $100

SMITH, F.L. Buttonlock, 3½" closed, nickel-silver liners and bolsters, osage orange scales, serial #8 $180

SMITH, F.L. Buttonlock in the style of Ron Richards or Bob Hayes, 4" closed, nickel-silver liners, bolsters, cocobolo scales, serial #4 .... $200

SMITH, F.L. Buttonlock, 4" closed, nickel-silver liners and bolsters, rosewood scales serial #9 $275

SMITH, JOHN T. Bootknife, 4⅛" blade, nickel-silver fittings, African blackwood handle and sheath, the best bootknife by a leading maker of 20 years ago $445

SMITH, JOHN T. Bootknife, 4¼" blade, brass hilt, ivory Micarta handle, John T. originated this style, has retired $195

SMITH, JOHN T. Dagger, 4⅛" blade, brass hilt, burgundy Micarta handle $265

SMITH, R.L. Bootknife, 4⅜" single-edged blade, stainless steel bolsters and pins, exotic wood handle $145

SMITH, RALPH Mini-skinner, 2¾" 154CM blade, stainless hilt and pins, cocobolo scales, very nice $105

SMITH, TOM (CANADA) Camp bowie, 9⅛" flat ground blade, hand-rubbed finish and fileworked back, nickel-silver hilt and pins, ivory Micarta handle scrimmed with lady's bust $485

SMITH, TOM (CANADA) Hunter, 3⅝" blade, nickel-silver hilt and sheath trim, crown stag handle, stag sheath $395

SMITH & WESSON 1975 6" blade, brass hilt and butt, wood Micarta handle, steamboat scene engraved blade, serial #8, no sheath $235

SMITH & WESSON 1975 5⅝" blade hunter, elephants engraved in blade, brass hilt and butt, wood Micarta hollow handle, serial #8, no sheath $195

SMITH & WESSON Texas Ranger Commemorative Bowie, 5¾" blade, brass hilt and butt, Wessonwood handle, no sheath, presentation box $175

SMITH & WESSON Texas Ranger Commemorative Bowie, 5⅞" blade, brass hilt and butt, Wessonwood handle, no sheath, presentation box $195

SMITH & WESSON Drop point, 5½" blade, brass hilt and butt cap to the hollow Wessonwood handle, box $165

SMITH & WESSON Drop point, 5½" blade, sterling silver hilt, butt and inlay cast with oak leaves, Wessonwood handles, Presentation Series #302 box, very rare $375

SMITH & WESSON Lockback, 4½" closed, nickel-silver bolsters, brass liners, wood Micarta slabs, used, black leather belt sheath $70

SMITH & WESSON Lockback, 4½" closed, nickel-silver bolsters, brass liners, wood Micarta scales, sheath, box, new $165

SMITH & WESSON Lockback, 4¾" closed, stainless interframe, rosewood inlays, belt pouch $25

SMITH & WESSON Skinner, 3½" blade, brass hilt, nickel-silver inlay, cracked wood handle ... $120

SMOKEY MOUNTAIN Clasp, 5½" closed, Mountaineer 1979-1 etched blade, nickel-silver bolsters, caps and inlay, bone scales, 1 of 600, serial #265 .... $40

SMOKEY MOUNTAIN Clasp, 5½" closed, Warrior 1980-3 etched blade, nickel-silver bolsters, caps and inlay, brass liners, rosewood scales, 1 of 600, serial #455 .... $35

SMOKEY MT. KNIFE WORKS Sleeveboard jack, 3⅝" blade etched Fight'n Cocks 190/600, stainless engraved Fight'n Rooster handle, brass liners $65

SOG Tigershark Bowie, 9" satin-finish blade, black rubber handle, new $110

SONNEVILLE Dagger, 7" blade, stainless hilt and butt, brown canvas Micarta handle $195

SORNBERGER Clip point, 4¼" 154CM, very tapered tang, engraved nickel-silver hilt, black liners, mother of pearl slab handle $385

SORNBERGER Drop point, 2¾" 154CM blade, stainless bolsters, tapered tang, ivory scales, sheath has broken snap $175

SPARKS Bird, 3¼" blade, stainless bolsters, stag scales $175

SPARKS Drop point, 3¾" blade, nickel-silver bolster and handle wrap, brass pins, rosewood handle, prominent late 60s and early 70s maker $220

SPARKS Lockback, 4¾" closed, brass liners and bolsters, wood Micarta scales $165

SPARKS Choked-up drop point skinner, 3⅛" stainless bolsters and pins, burgundy Micarta scales, skinner, shows Bernard's trapper background, great for close-in tight work $220

SPENCER Drop point hunter, 3½" engraved hollow-ground blade, coral liners, stag slabs $95

SPENCER Single-blade slipjoint, 4" closed, nickel-silver bolsters and liners, exotic wood scales $95

SPRATT'S (ENGLAND) Two-blade jack (sheepsfoot and a blade for stripping dogs' coats, I believe), 3½" closed, nickel-silver bolsters, brass liners, jigged bone scales, used, very good $75

STANDARD CUTLERY Ladies' dagger, 4½" nickel-silver hilt, walrus age-cracked ivory handle, pocket sheath missing tip, over 100 years old $95

STAPEL Skinner, 3¾" blade, ivory Micarta scales, scrimmed javelina on handle $75

STEVE'S KNIVES 5½" blade, very rough brass hilt, rosewood handle, no sheath, very early $45

STEWART, CHUCK Buttonlock, 4" closed, stainless interframe, rosewood inlay, new $495

STEWART, CHUCK Stainless interframe linerlock, 3¼" closed, satin-finish 154CM stainless steel blade, Rockwell hardness rating RC 58-60, beautiful pink pearl inlays, mint $245

STIDHAM'S Cigar whittler, 4½" closed, nickel-silver bolsters dog's head inlay, brass liners, stag scales $55

STODDART Skinner, 3" blade, wood Micarta scales $45

STONE Bird and trout, 4" blade, brass hilt and butt, leather handle $145

STONE Fighter, 8" satin-finish blade marked A135, brass hilt and butt, stag handle, new $335

STONE Fish fillet, 6" stainless blade, stag scales $175

STONE Skinner, 5" blade, brass hilt and butt, brown Micarta handle $255

STONE Mini-skinner, 2" blade, all steel $85

STONE Mini-skinner, 2" all steel MS12S satin-finish blade, leather belt sheath $90

STRONG Dropped clip point skinner, 5" black blade, black Micarta scales $125

T

TAPIO WIRKKALA/HACKMAN (FINLAND) 4" stainless blade, brass hilt and butt, black Micarta handle $40

TAYLOR, C. GRAY Lobster, 2⅜" closed, satin-finish blade, stainless interframe, black pearl inlay, very nice, see page 82 Knives '86 .... $385

TAYLOR, G. Drop point, 3¾" blade, engraved, brass hilt and pins, ivory Micarta scales, early work by fine maker $75

TAYLOR, G. Pen letter opener, 2⅞" mirror-finish blade, wood sheath $145

TAYLOR CUTLERY (JAPAN) Copperhead lockback, 3¾" closed, brass liners, nickel-silver bolsters, pearl scales, original box, new $40

TAYLOR CUTLERY (JAPAN) Lockback, 3½" closed, nickel-silver bolsters and caps, brass liners, pearl, scales abalone inlay $30

TAYLOR CUTLERY (JAPAN) Lockback, 3⅝" closed, surgical steel blade, brass liners, nickel-silver bolsters pearl and abalone scales, new $40

TAYLOR EYE WITNESS (ENGLAND) 4⅞" finn blade, brass hilt, aluminum butt, stag handle, old but little used $40

TEKNA Security card knife, 3⅜" closed, stainless blade, plastic credit-card-shaped handle, in case, new $25

TERRILL Bootknife, 5½" Loveless-style blade, mirror-finish, nickel-silver hilt and pins, black liners, ivory Micarta scales, tapered tang, #137, little used $295

TERZUOLA (GUATEMALA) 4¾" blade, bead blasted pins and blade, brown Micarta slabs $275

TERZUOLA (GUATEMALA) Model 26 Queen Susan fighter, 5⅛" satin-finish 440C stainless 59 RC Rockwell hardness blade, stainless pins and thong hole, red spacers, black Micarta scales, original box, new $275

TERZUOLA (GUATEMALA) Small fighter, 5" blade, black Micarta handle, locking Kydex sheath, used $165

TERZUOLA (GUATEMALA) Fighter, 5½" bead-blasted blade, black Micarta handle, used .. $215

TERZUOLA (GUATEMALA) Fighter, 5¾" blade, black Micarta handle, locking Kydex sheath, used $185

TERZUOLA (GUATEMALA) Fighter, 6" bead-blasted blade, black Micarta scales, formed Kydex sheath, very nice $295

TERZUOLA (GUATEMALA) Fighter, 6½" blade, black Micarta handle, bead blasted, used .. $195

TERZUOLA (GUATEMALA) Model 12 fighter, 4¾" bead-blasted D-2 blade, ziracote wood handle, Kydex sheath $375

TERZUOLA (GUATEMALA) Model SJ-2 Smoke Jumpers, 3½" bead-blasted D-2-steel blade, black Micarta scales, Kydex sheath $65

TERZUOLA (SANTA FE, NM) Linerlock, 3½" closed, bead-blasted titanium handle and blade, all metal, very nice $365

KNIFE COLLECTORS CLUB, THE Complete set CM-1 through CM-12, includes CM-3 Special and FH-1, all serial #1376 .... $835

THOMASON Dagger, 5½" blade, nickel-silver hilt, filework tang, ivory Micarta scales $155

THOMPSON Drop point hunter, 3" blade, nickel silver hilt, ivory Micarta scales, superb grind and polish, the best work I have seen from this maker, hilt and handle engraved by Mel Woods $200

THOMPSON Lockback, 3½" closed, mirror-finish 154CM blade, stainless bolsters, liners, and pins, red jigged bone scales $235

THOMPSON-CENTER Three-blade stock, 3¼" closed, stainless steel bolsters, brass liners, rosewood scales, very rare $190

THOMPSON-CENTER Three-blade stock, 4¼" closed, stainless steel bolsters, brass liners, rosewood scales, rare $175

THOMPSON, L.J. Lockback, satin-finish blade, 3½" closed, stainless bolsters, thong hole and liners, burgundy Micarta slabs, mint $245

THORNTON Survival, 4 7/16" blade, stainless hilt, alloy tube handle, unmarked, one of the earliest—after Randall and Bourne—hollow-handles, no sheath $165

THORNTON 1979 Quicksilver survival, satin-finish blade, hollow aluminum handle $95

TIGER (GERMANY) Two-blade carpenter, 3⅝" closed, screw driver and door knob tool, shadow pattern ivory celluloid scales, handle engraved D. Barnette Tool Co., Newark, N.J. $115

TIMBERLINE 3¼" sawtooth-back blade, xotic wood scales $345

TIMBERLINE Little fighter, 3¼" bead-blasted blade, black Micarta scales $395

TIMBERLINE Tanto, 5¾" blade, steel bolster and butt, black Micarta handle $150

TIMBERLINE Tanto, 7½" blade, steel hilt and butt, black Micarta handle $225

TINKER, CAROLINE Skinner, 3½" 154CM stainless blade, nickel-silver hilt, African blackwood handles $80

TOKAR Hunter, 4" blade, brass hilt and butt, rosewood handle $55

TOMES Bowie, 9" damascus blade, engraved, nickel-silver hilt and butt, oosic handle, no sheath, zipper case, very nice $575

TOMES Drop point, 3⅜" blade, stainless steel hilt, stag scales, very nice flat and little $175

TOWELL Bowie, 8¾" blade, nickel-silver hilt and inlay, rosewood slabs, leather sheath with fitted nickel-silver, early work by a great maker ... $485

TOWELL Lockback, 4⅛" closed, hollow-ground mirror-finish blade, nickel-silver bolsters, liners and pins, curly maple scales $395

TOWELL Lockback, 4⅝" closed, brass liners and bolster, stag scales $255

TOWELL Semi-skinner Model 12, 3½" 154CM blade, nickel-silver hilt, tapered tang, desert ironwood scales, fantastic—from one of the masters $395

TRABBIC, R. Drop point, 3¾" blade, nieckel-silver hilt and butt cap, coral and white spacers, stag handle $150

TRACK Bowie, 5½" blade, engraved 75th Grand American August 23, 1974 Dr. Jack Marvich, Serial No 201 of 750, nickel-silver hilt, rosewood handle $135

TRU-BAL Thrower, 8¾" blade, brass hilt, black handle, used $30

TRU-BAL Thrower, 9⅛" blade, black fiber handle $25

TRU-BAL Thrower, 13½" blade, all-steel $25

TURNBULL Slim drop point, 3½" blade, brass hilt and pins, burgundy and black Micarta scales $75

TURNBULL Filet, 7¼" mirror-finish blade, brass hilt and pins, black Micarta slabs $115

TURNBULL Lockback, 3" closed, beautiful rose pattern damascus blade, stainless frames, ebony scales with black pearl inlays, unmarked ... $295

U

USMC Four-blade pocket, 3¾″ closed, marked USA, jigged bone scales pre-WW II $75
U.S. Bayonet, steel hilt and butt, wood inlay handle, DP engraved in hilt and handle, no sheath . . . $35
U.S. Eighteenth century socket bayonet, 18″ blade, all steel, no sheath $35
U.S. 1899 Krag bayonet, 11½″ blade, fuller on both sides, steel hilt and butt, wood handles, steel sheath, very good $45
U.S. 1912 Bolo, 10½″ blade, iron hilt, butt, wood handle, sharpened and used $75
ULSTER Two-blade even-end pen, 2¼″ closed, nickel-silver bolsters, brass liners, fine mother of pearl scales, used $40
UNION CUTLERY CO. (OLEAN, NY) Clip point skinner, 5″ blade, steel hilt, jigged wood scales, very used $25
UNKNOWN (GERMANY) Two-blade and corkscrew champagne, 3¼″ closed, horn celluloid scales, circus pony trademark $35
UNKNOWN (GERMANY) Traveler's dining set, Morocco leather case containing a heavy glass drinking glass holding folding knife and fork, brass liners and white celluloid scales, the only one of these I have ever seen $145
UNKNOWN WW II, 6″ blade, brass hilt and butt, leather handle, no sheath $60
UNKNOWN WW II dagger, 6¼″ blade, brass hilt and butt, plexiglas handle $70
UNKNOWN COUNTRY 8½″ blade, brass fittings, cattle horn handle carved into a dog's head $50
UNMARKED Bowie, 14½″ forged blade, steel hilt, wood handle, no sheath (Owner thought this a Confederate Bowie, it could be, very rough work and it is, in my opinion, at least 50 years old $225
UNMARKED Brass knucklebuster, 8½″ triangular blade, D-hilt, split wood handle, no sheath, home made, WW II?, home made $75

V

VALACHOVIC 7" blade, steel hilt and butt, rosewood handle, light pitting on blade $265

VALACHOVIC 9½" forged high carbon steel blade, fileworked back, steel hilt and butt spike, stag handle, D-ring sheath $445

VALACHOVIC Bowie, 9½" forged high carbon steel blade, hilt and butt, India stag handle, used a little, fine work from one of the very best smiths $365

VALACHOVIC Bowie, 10" High Density Damascus (22,000 layers) blade, damascus roped hilt and butt, maple handle, an absolutely fantastic show piece and the last straight knife Wayne made, he makes only folders now, no other like it $2,785

VALOCHOVIC Dagger, 4⅛" damascus blade, damascus hilt, India stag handle $355

VALACHOVIC Fighter, 5" blade, steel hilt and butt, birdseye maple handle $185

VALACHOVIC Fighter, 5⅜" blade, steel hilt, rosewood handle $145

VALACHOVIC Ashokan fighter, 6⅞" fileworked blade, steel hilt, cocobolo handle $275

VALACHOVIC Clip point fighter, 8" forged blade, nickel-silver hilt and butt cap, cocobolo handle $485

VALACHOVIC Hunter, 3½" blade, bone Micarta handle $125

VALACHOVIC Tail-lock right-hand stud opener, 3" closed, damascus steel blade, liners and bolsters, pink mother-of-pearl scales $700

VALOIS Fighter, 7" bead-blasted blade, hilt and tang, wood Micarta slabs, new $225

VALOIS, AD Folder (some mechanisms should never have been made), 4⅝" closed, stainless bolsters and liners, wood Micarta and turquoise slabs, new $100

VALOR Folder, 5⅛" closed, stainless blade, bolster and liners, plastic pearl scales $25

VENTURE (SHEFFIELD) Bowie, 5⅞" pitted blade, brass hilt, stag scales rough shape $40

VICTORINOX Abercrombie & Fitch slipjoint—blade, nail file, scissors, toothpick and tweezers—2¼" closed, black plastic scales, brass inlay both sides, ... $25

VICTORINOX Two-blade sleeveboard lobster, 3″ closed, stainless liners and blade, beautiful pearl scales, very slim, new $75

VIELE Bootknife, 3″ blade, nickel-silver hilt, ivory Micarta scales, armor piercing point $185

VIELE Caper, 3″ blade, ivory Micarta scales, buffalo scrimmed one side $115

VOSS Stillson wrench and pocket tool kit—gimlet, reamer, screwdriver, file and knife blade—4⅛″ closed, chrome plated steel handles, very rare, very fine $295

VOSS CUTLERY (GERMANY) Three-blade Wharncliffe whittler, 3½″ closed, nickel-silver bolsters and inlay, brass liners, stag scales, used $135

VOSS CUTLERY (GERMANY) Four-blade congress, 3⅝″ closed, nickel-silver bolsters, brass liners, fine pearl scales $115

VOUGHT Bowie, 9″ blade, brass hilt, stag handles $295

VOUGHT Drop point, 3¼″ blade, sterling silver trim, abalone inlays, no sheath, would make a beautiful letter opener $265

VOUGHT Fighter, 5½″ blade, black Micarta scales $125

W

WAGNER, W. (GERMANY) Two-blade pocket, 3¼″ closed, nickel-silver bolsters, brass liners, fine pearl handle, beautiful, slim $125

WADE & BUTCHER (GERMANY) Four-blade congress, 3⅝″ closed, nickel-silver bolsters, brass liners, stag scales $70

WADE & BUTCHER Three-blade congress, 3¾″ closed, nickel-silver bolsters, pins and liners, stag slabs $65

WADE & BUTCHER (SHEFFIELD) Razor, 6″ engraved blade, horn scales $24

WAHLSTER, M. 3″ bead-blasted ATS34 steel blade, stainless pins, blue pacawood scales $75

WAKIZASHI Sword, 17″ etched blade, engraved butt, black hilt, blue and gold dragons onlay, black cord wrapped handle, orange sheath with matching onlays $150

WALDEN Lockback, 3¾" closed, brass bolsters and pins, burgundy linen Micarta scales, 1980 .. $140

WARENSKI Drop point, 4" blade, brass hilt, butt, rosewood handle $295

WARENSKI, BUSTER Drop point, 3½" 154CM blade, hand-rubbed nickel-silver bolsters engraved by Lynton McKenzie, ivory scales wonderfully scrimmed by Buster, crack on one side, no sheath, outstanding piece once in Blevins collection $1,895

WARENSKI, BUSTER Hunter, 4" blade, brass hilt, black Micarta handle, early $295

WARENSKI/PRICE (CALIFORNIA) Bowie, 6⅝" blade, nickel-silver trim on ivory handle and sheath $1345

WARENSKI/PRICE (CALIFORNIA) California dagger, 5½" blade, nickel-silver trim on ivory handle and scabbard $845

WATSON, RED Caper, 2¾" blade, brass hilt and butt cap, ivory Micarta handle $175

WATSON, RED Skinner, 4" blade, stag scales $175

WEBER 5½" mirror-finish blade, tapered tang, red liners, nickel-silver hilt, pins and thong hole, African blackwood slabs, new $175

WEBBER Fighter, 6" blade, nickel-silver hilt, ironwood handle $195

WEBER, F. Drop point, 3¾" blade, nickel-silver hilt, ivory Micarta scales, #3 .... $135

WEBER, F.E. Bootknife, 4⅛" blade, tapered tang, red liners, ivory Micarta scales, new $155

WEBSTER WOOD 5⅛" bead-blasted blade, green, red and black wood Micarta handle $65

WEILER 7" upswept pitted blade, nickel-silver hilt and butt, wood slabs, used $115

WEILER 8½" upswept blade, nickel-silver hilt, rosewood slabs, blade pitted, no sheath, used .. $115

WEILER Bootknife, 5½" blade, brass hilt, wood handle with steel lace $235

WEILER Bowie, 7" blued steel blade, hilt and butt, black Micarta scales $185

WEILER Drop point, 3¾" blade, nickel-silver hilt and butt, twisted wirewrap tang, ironwood scales $165

WEILER American straight edge fighter, 5" blade, black and brown Micarta handle, used $125

WEILER American straight edge fighter, 7½" blade, black and brown Micarta handle $145

WEILER Drop point fighter, 7½" blade, stainless pins, black Micarta slabs, used $95

WEILER Hunter, 3½" blade, nickel-silver hilt and pins, ironwood scales $155

WEILER Drop point, hunter, 4" blade, brass hilt, butt cap and pins, desert ironwood handle $140

WEILER Lockback, 4¼" closed, fileworked blade and brass liners, nickel-silver bolsters, ironwood scales $125

WEILER American scramasax, 7" blade, black Micarta handles $135

WEILER Scramasax, 13½" blade, nickel-silver hilt and butt, ironwood handle, a very nice Weiler, turquoise in butt $330

WEILER Skean dhu, 4" blade, brass bolster, cocobolo scales, carved $165

WEILER Skean dhu, large 5¾" blade, brass bolster and butt, ironwood carved like braided leather, very nice $275

WEIMAN Two-blade slipjoint, 5¼" closed, steel liners and bolsters, brown Micarta scales, Bob Ludwig style $85

WELCH Belt, 2½" stainless drop point blade, ivory Micarta scales, serial #25 .... $115

WELCH Shirt pocket, 3¼" blade, ivory Micarta scales $95

WENOKA Bootknife, 2⅜" stainless blade, black rubber handle and sheath $35

WERCO 600 tomahawk, hickory handle, made from the head of a German hatchet, no sheath $55

WESTERN Combat, 6" blade with fullers, brass hilt, aluminum butt, leather handle, circa WW II, used $115

WESTERN Lockback, 4¼" closed, nickel-silver engraved bolsters and caps, brass liners, ivory scales, leather belt pouch $140

WESTERN Skinner, 4⅞" blade, aluminum hilt and butt, four-piece stag handle, used $50

WESTERN STATES CUTLERY Razor, 6" closed, celluloid scales $20

WEYERSBERG KIRSHBAUM & CO. (SOLINGEN) 10" blade with fuller both sides, metal and leather sheath, chrome plated when new, date unknown $55

WILBER Bootknife, 3¼" blade, nickel-silver bolster and pins, blackwood scales $240

WILBER, W.C. Slipjoint, 3⅝″ closed, stainless bolsters and liners, black Micarta scales, very hard-to-find $145

WILD BILL & SONS Fighter, 6¼″ satin-finish blade, nickel-silver hilt, wood handle, used $265

WILDING Drop point, 3½″ 154CM blade, stainless hilt, brown Micarta scales $115

WILKINSON SWORD (ENGLAND) Airborne commemorative dagger, 6⅞″ blade, brass hilt, brass handle, celebrates WW II Normandy landings $155

WILKINSON SWORD (ENGLAND) Commando commemorative dagger, 7″ blade, steel hilt, lead handle plated in gold, #31 of 500, no sheath, special presentation box $155

WILKINSON SWORD (ENGLAND) Battle of Britain Commemorative dagger, 10¾″ blade, gold-plated hilt, butt, ivory plastic, leather sheath with gold-plated trim, display box $265

WILLIAM, W.C. Slipjoint, 3½″ closed, brass interframe, rosewood inlays $150

WILLIAMS, ALFRED (ENGLAND) Bowie, 7″ blade, nickel-silver hilt, stag scales, no sheath, old $65

WILSON, E. (ENGLAND) Sticker, 6″ double shear steel hand forged blade, wood handle, no sheath $20

WILSON, R.W. Green River skinner, 4⅛″ blade, tapered tang, brass hilt, curly maple slabs $145

WILSON (ITALY) Miniature Buckmaster, 4¾″ overall, 2⅞″ blade, outstanding $45

WIMAN 3½″ blade, brass hilt and butt, osage orange scales, too long sheath $65

WIMAN Drop point, 3⅞″ blade, brass hilt and pins, stag scales, hilt epoxy on one side $50

WIMAN Hunter, 4″ blade, brass hilt, nickel-silver arrowhead onlay, mortise tang, stag handle $75

WINCHESTER Lockback, 4″ closed, tarnished nickel-silver bolsters, ivory delrin scales, satin-finish blade etched, cowboy on horse on handle ... $30

WINCHESTER Lockback, Model 1927, 5⅜″ closed, nickel-silver bolsters and inlay, brass liners, peach seed bone scales, mismarked 1950, made in 1988, the factory mismarked some of the first of this model made $90

WINCHESTER Two-blade senator, 3¼″ closed, nickel-silver tips and inlay, brass liners, blue-green pearl celluloid scales, used and pitted, little wear $35

WINCHESTER Toothpick, 4¼" closed, etched blade, nickel-silver bolsters and inlay, brass liners, jigged bone scales $35

WINCHESTER (GERMANY) Bootleg two-blade muskrat, 4" closed, blade etched in black and gold WINCHESTER Muskrat 1 of 1000, no serial number, nickel-silver bolsters and inlay, brass liners and pins, igged bone scales, not marked Germany, ... $55

WINGEN, ANTON (GERMANY) D.F. Kressler design clip point, 4" blade, integral hilt, tapered tang, burgundy Micarta scales, very fine $125

WINGEN, ANTON (GERMANY) Clip point bootknife, 4" single edge blade, integral hilt and butt, stag scales, nice metal trimmed pocket sheath $125

WINGEN, ANTON (GERMANY) Six steak knives and six forks, color etched outdoor scene blades, hand-carved India stag handles, very nice set, a storage case $285

WINKLER 5⅝" blade, brass hilt, antler handle, used $95

WINKLER 8" forged blade, hand-rubbed finish, stainless hilt and pins, nicely matched stag handle $175

W K Hunter, 6" blade, nickel-silver hilt, butt, stag handle $275

W K Hunter, 6½ blade, nickel-silver hilt and butt, India stag handle, sharpened, mountain man sheath covered in brass tacks $225

WOOD, BARRY MK I swivel-lock, 4¼" closed, brown Micarta scales, mint $385

WOOD, BARRY MK I swivel-lock, 4½" closed, burgundy Micarta scales, serial #78 .... $675

WOOD, BARRY Swivel-lock, 3¾" closed, satin-finish stainless steel blade, cordura sheath, #4, new $145

WOOD, BARRY (PACIFIC CUTLERY) Swivel-lock, 3⅝" closed, satin-finished blade, stainless steel handle $60

WOOD, BARRY MK IV, 4⅜" closed, bronze frames, ebony inlays, serial #182 .... $795

WOOD, OWEN (SOUTH AFRICA) Drop point, 3⅜" 440C blade, nickel-silver bolster, African blackwood scales, very nice $155

WORM Slipjoint, 3¼" closed, engraved bolster, ivory Micarta scales, bird engraved on handle, serial #47, early work $100

WORM Folder, 3⅜" blade, stainless hilt, stag slabs $275

WORM Leon M. Pittman folder, 3½" closed, D-2 steel blade, stainless bolsters and liners, smooth stag slabs, made 1982 .... $225

WORM Pittman pocket dagger, 3¼" closed, nickel-silver bolsters, steel frame, rosewood scales $295

WOSTENHOLM 1985 Limited Edition five-blade congress, 3½" closed, nickel-silver bolsters, black pearl scales, serial #1688 .... $60

WOSTENHOLM (JAPAN) American Blade 1985 six -blade congress, 3½" closed, nickel-silver bolsters, brass liners, black pearl scales, #1226 of 5000 $65

WOSTENHOLM CUTLERY Box of five unfinished senator whittlers, ABC brass liners, no bolsters, original box $250

WRAGE (ENGLAND) Single clip blade, nickel-silver bolsters, stag coke bottle handle $35

WRENCH Bowie, 6" blade, brass hilt and butt, stag handle $125

WRENCH Bowie, 6" blade, brass hilt and butt, wood Micarta handle $95

WRENCH Abercrombie & Fitch bowie, 5¾" blade, brass hilt and butt, India stag handle $165

WRIGHT, TIM Bird, 3¼" blade, tapered tang, stainless hilt, pearl inlay desert ironwood scales, in Knives 89 .... $195

WYOMING Swivel-lock, 4¾" closed, mirror-finish blade, all stainless, belt sheath $35

X

X/B Patch, 5½" blade, nickel-silver butt and bolster, small pearl inlay, ebony handle, maker in Ohio in the 60s named Bourne $245

Y

YANCEY Bootknife, 4⅜" blade, brass single hilt and pins, ivory Rucarta scales scrimmed by Ann Yancey $275

YANCEY Dagger, 6⅛" 154CM blade, brass hilt, zytel handle with weights inside for balance, the original handmade version of the Applegate-Fairbairn and by far the best, few made because of misunderstandings between the people involved $395

YANCEY Drop point, 4" blade, brass hilt, burgundy Micarta scales $195

YANCEY Drop point, 4" blade, brass hilt and pins, ivory Micarta handles with eagle scrimmed by Ann Yancey $375

YANCEY Fighter, 5" engraved blade, engraved brass hilt, ivory scales with scrimmed Roman soldier $395

YANCEY Guthook, 3⅛" mirror-finish blade, tapered tang, brass hilt and pins, ivory Micarta slabs, quail in field scrimmed by Ann Yancey, #414 .... $395

YANCEY Straight hunter, 5" blade, brass hilt and pins, ivory Micarta handles scrimmed in color by Ann Yancey, no sheath, tree trunk box $285

YANCEY Fifteen hunters in three glass-covered frames, nickel-silver hilts, ivory Micarta scales, great color scrimshaw by Ann Yancey, one of two sets made, less than original cost $5,295

YANCEY Skinner, 4" mirror-polish blade, brass hilt and pins, tapered tang, red liners, ivory Micarta scales, very fine scrimmed deer, new $295

Z

ZACHERY 3⅞" blade, stainless bolsters, cocobolo handle $125

ZACK 3½" blade, brass trim, sculpted brass and yellow Micarta handle, no sheath $265

ZACK Upswept skinner, 5¼" hand-rubbed blade, butt and double hilt of stainless steel, three-piece finger-groove rosewood handle, unused ... $295

KNIFE RECORD

MAKE/DESCRIPTION

DATE/SELLER/PRICE

DATE/BUYER/PRICE

MAKE/DESCRIPTION

DATE/SELLER/PRICE

DATE/BUYER/PRICE

MAKE/DESCRIPTION

DATE/SELLER/PRICE

DATE/BUYER/PRICE

MAKE/DESCRIPTION

DATE/SELLER/PRICE

DATE/BUYER/PRICE

MAKE/DESCRIPTION

DATE/SELLER/PRICE

DATE/BUYER/PRICE

MAKE/DESCRIPTION

DATE/SELLER/PRICE

DATE/BUYER/PRICE

Use ball-point pen

KNIFE RECORD

MAKE/DESCRIPTION

DATE/SELLER/PRICE

DATE/BUYER/PRICE

MAKE/DESCRIPTION

DATE/SELLER/PRICE

DATE/BUYER/PRICE

MAKE/DESCRIPTION

DATE/SELLER/PRICE

DATE/BUYER/PRICE

MAKE/DESCRIPTION

DATE/SELLER/PRICE

DATE/BUYER/PRICE

MAKE/DESCRIPTION

DATE/SELLER/PRICE

DATE/BUYER/PRICE

MAKE/DESCRIPTION

DATE/SELLER/PRICE

DATE/BUYER/PRICE

Use ball-point pen

KNIFE RECORD

MAKE/DESCRIPTION

DATE/SELLER/PRICE

DATE/BUYER/PRICE

MAKE/DESCRIPTION

DATE/SELLER/PRICE

DATE/BUYER/PRICE

MAKE/DESCRIPTION

DATE/SELLER/PRICE

DATE/BUYER/PRICE

MAKE/DESCRIPTION

DATE/SELLER/PRICE

DATE/BUYER/PRICE

MAKE/DESCRIPTION

DATE/SELLER/PRICE

DATE/BUYER/PRICE

MAKE/DESCRIPTION

DATE/SELLER/PRICE

DATE/BUYER/PRICE

Use ball-point pen

KNIFE RECORD

MAKE/DESCRIPTION

DATE/SELLER/PRICE

DATE/BUYER/PRICE

MAKE/DESCRIPTION

DATE/SELLER/PRICE

DATE/BUYER/PRICE

MAKE/DESCRIPTION

DATE/SELLER/PRICE

DATE/BUYER/PRICE

MAKE/DESCRIPTION

DATE/SELLER/PRICE

DATE/BUYER/PRICE

MAKE/DESCRIPTION

DATE/SELLER/PRICE

DATE/BUYER/PRICE

MAKE/DESCRIPTION

DATE/SELLER/PRICE

DATE/BUYER/PRICE

Use ball-point pen

© 1991 PWC

KNIFE RECORD

MAKE/DESCRIPTION

DATE/SELLER/PRICE

DATE/BUYER/PRICE

MAKE/DESCRIPTION

DATE/SELLER/PRICE

DATE/BUYER/PRICE

MAKE/DESCRIPTION

DATE/SELLER/PRICE

DATE/BUYER/PRICE

MAKE/DESCRIPTION

DATE/SELLER/PRICE

DATE/BUYER/PRICE

MAKE/DESCRIPTION

DATE/SELLER/PRICE

DATE/BUYER/PRICE

MAKE/DESCRIPTION

DATE/SELLER/PRICE

DATE/BUYER/PRICE

Use ball-point pen

KNIFE RECORD

MAKE/DESCRIPTION

DATE/SELLER/PRICE

DATE/BUYER/PRICE

MAKE/DESCRIPTION

DATE/SELLER/PRICE

DATE/BUYER/PRICE

MAKE/DESCRIPTION

DATE/SELLER/PRICE

DATE/BUYER/PRICE

MAKE/DESCRIPTION

DATE/SELLER/PRICE

DATE/BUYER/PRICE

MAKE/DESCRIPTION

DATE/SELLER/PRICE

DATE/BUYER/PRICE

MAKE/DESCRIPTION

DATE/SELLER/PRICE

DATE/BUYER/PRICE

Use ball-point pen

KNIFE RECORD

MAKE/DESCRIPTION

DATE/SELLER/PRICE

DATE/BUYER/PRICE

MAKE/DESCRIPTION

DATE/SELLER/PRICE

DATE/BUYER/PRICE

MAKE/DESCRIPTION

DATE/SELLER/PRICE

DATE/BUYER/PRICE

MAKE/DESCRIPTION

DATE/SELLER/PRICE

DATE/BUYER/PRICE

MAKE/DESCRIPTION

DATE/SELLER/PRICE

DATE/BUYER/PRICE

MAKE/DESCRIPTION

DATE/SELLER/PRICE

DATE/BUYER/PRICE

Use ball-point pen

© 1991 PWC

KNIFE RECORD

MAKE/DESCRIPTION

DATE/SELLER/PRICE

DATE/BUYER/PRICE

MAKE/DESCRIPTION

DATE/SELLER/PRICE

DATE/BUYER/PRICE

MAKE/DESCRIPTION

DATE/SELLER/PRICE

DATE/BUYER/PRICE

MAKE/DESCRIPTION

DATE/SELLER/PRICE

DATE/BUYER/PRICE

MAKE/DESCRIPTION

DATE/SELLER/PRICE

DATE/BUYER/PRICE

MAKE/DESCRIPTION

DATE/SELLER/PRICE

DATE/BUYER/PRICE

Use ball-point pen

KNIFE RECORD

MAKE/DESCRIPTION

DATE/SELLER/PRICE

DATE/BUYER/PRICE

MAKE/DESCRIPTION

DATE/SELLER/PRICE

DATE/BUYER/PRICE

MAKE/DESCRIPTION

DATE/SELLER/PRICE

DATE/BUYER/PRICE

MAKE/DESCRIPTION

DATE/SELLER/PRICE

DATE/BUYER/PRICE

MAKE/DESCRIPTION

DATE/SELLER/PRICE

DATE/BUYER/PRICE

MAKE/DESCRIPTION

DATE/SELLER/PRICE

DATE/BUYER/PRICE

Use ball-point pen

KNIFE RECORD

MAKE/DESCRIPTION

DATE/SELLER/PRICE

DATE/BUYER/PRICE

MAKE/DESCRIPTION

DATE/SELLER/PRICE

DATE/BUYER/PRICE

MAKE/DESCRIPTION

DATE/SELLER/PRICE

DATE/BUYER/PRICE

MAKE/DESCRIPTION

DATE/SELLER/PRICE

DATE/BUYER/PRICE

MAKE/DESCRIPTION

DATE/SELLER/PRICE

DATE/BUYER/PRICE

MAKE/DESCRIPTION

DATE/SELLER/PRICE

DATE/BUYER/PRICE

Use ball-point pen

KNIFE RECORD

MAKE/DESCRIPTION

DATE/SELLER/PRICE

DATE/BUYER/PRICE

MAKE/DESCRIPTION

DATE/SELLER/PRICE

DATE/BUYER/PRICE

MAKE/DESCRIPTION

DATE/SELLER/PRICE

DATE/BUYER/PRICE

MAKE/DESCRIPTION

DATE/SELLER/PRICE

DATE/BUYER/PRICE

MAKE/DESCRIPTION

DATE/SELLER/PRICE

DATE/BUYER/PRICE

MAKE/DESCRIPTION

DATE/SELLER/PRICE

DATE/BUYER/PRICE

Use ball-point pen

KNIFE RECORD

MAKE/DESCRIPTION

DATE/SELLER/PRICE

DATE/BUYER/PRICE

MAKE/DESCRIPTION

DATE/SELLER/PRICE

DATE/BUYER/PRICE

MAKE/DESCRIPTION

DATE/SELLER/PRICE

DATE/BUYER/PRICE

MAKE/DESCRIPTION

DATE/SELLER/PRICE

DATE/BUYER/PRICE

MAKE/DESCRIPTION

DATE/SELLER/PRICE

DATE/BUYER/PRICE

MAKE/DESCRIPTION

DATE/SELLER/PRICE

DATE/BUYER/PRICE

Use ball-point pen

KNIFE RECORD

MAKE/DESCRIPTION

DATE/SELLER/PRICE

DATE/BUYER/PRICE

MAKE/DESCRIPTION

DATE/SELLER/PRICE

DATE/BUYER/PRICE

MAKE/DESCRIPTION

DATE/SELLER/PRICE

DATE/BUYER/PRICE

MAKE/DESCRIPTION

DATE/SELLER/PRICE

DATE/BUYER/PRICE

MAKE/DESCRIPTION

DATE/SELLER/PRICE

DATE/BUYER/PRICE

MAKE/DESCRIPTION

DATE/SELLER/PRICE

DATE/BUYER/PRICE

Use ball-point pen

KNIFE RECORD

MAKE/DESCRIPTION

DATE/SELLER/PRICE

DATE/BUYER/PRICE

MAKE/DESCRIPTION

DATE/SELLER/PRICE

DATE/BUYER/PRICE

MAKE/DESCRIPTION

DATE/SELLER/PRICE

DATE/BUYER/PRICE

MAKE/DESCRIPTION

DATE/SELLER/PRICE

DATE/BUYER/PRICE

MAKE/DESCRIPTION

DATE/SELLER/PRICE

DATE/BUYER/PRICE

MAKE/DESCRIPTION

DATE/SELLER/PRICE

DATE/BUYER/PRICE

Use ball-point pen

The Authors,
A. G. and Goldie Russell

WIDELY KNOWN AS "MR. KNIFE," native Arkansawyer A. G. Russell has been selling knives by mail for almost 30 years and is an acknowledged leader in his industry. *The Cutting Edge*, A. G.'s periodical publication which reaches tens of thousands of knife buffs, includes the consignment sales service, "List of Knives for Immediate Delivery," on which *Knife Trader's Guide* is based.

A founder of the Knifemakers Guild, A. G. Russell is its honorary president. In 1970, he formed the Knife Collectors Club, first American organization of its kind, and continues as the president. At the same time, A. G. designed and had made the earliest limited edition pocket knife, "The Kentucky Rifle." He rescued the Morseth handmade knife from impending extinction in 1971 and still produces it. From 1975 to 1980, Russell's help enabled Bertram, German maker of the fine Hen & Rooster pocket knives, to stave off bankruptcy.

A. G. not only sells knives, he designs, manufactures and imports them too. Probably his most famous product is the best-selling "CIA Letter Opener," of which perhaps 100,000 have been sold.

With his wife, Goldie, Russell attends most major knife shows nationwide. They personally know thousands of knife makers, dealers and collectors as friends and customers of their Springdale, Arkansas mail order business.

Goldie Russell is from Missouri. She started learning everything about the knife business by joining A. G. at shows and in frequent visits with makers and collectors. Six years later, she went to work for the A. G. Russell firm. Today, Goldie is the company's operations manager—proof of how knowledgeable she has become. Call her "Mrs. Knife."

If you're at a knife show and spot A. G. and Goldie, walk up to them and say "Howdy!".